JOB SEEKING

Also in the Career PowerTools Series

Plan Your Career by John Lockett

Powerful Networking by John Lockett

Thrive in Your Company by Hilton Catt and Patricia Scudamore

Get Headhunted by Hilton Catt and Patricia Scudamore

Interviews and Appraisals by Karen Holmes

JOB SEEKING

KAREN HOLMES

ORION BUSINESS
BOOKS

Copyright © 1999 by Karen Holmes

All rights reserved

The right of Karen Holmes to be identified as the author of this work has been asserted by her in accordance with the Copyright, Designs and Patents Act 1988.

First published in Great Britain in 1999 by
Orion Business
An imprint of
The Orion Publishing Group Ltd
Orion House
5 Upper St Martin's Lane
London WC2H 9EA

A CIP catalogue record for this book
is available from the British Library.

ISBN 0-75282-091-5

Typeset by Deltatype Ltd, Birkenhead
Printed and bound in Great Britain
by Clays Ltd, St Ives plc.

CONTENTS

INTRODUCTION 1

Part one STEPPING OUT

The job seeker   12
A systematic approach   19
The ideal job?   20
Seek expert advice   25
What can you offer?   25
Know yourself   27
Recruitment and selection   30
Recruitment   32
Selection   35
Searching for the right candidate   37
Summary   48

Part two STEPPING FORWARD

Your personal databank   52
Interpreting the advertisement   55
Responding to advertisements   59
Improving your written communication skills   60
Preparing the right CV   67
Application forms   78
Covering letters   83
Telephone skills   91
Summary   98

Part three STEP BY STEP

The interview process 102
Which style of interview 105
The stages of the interview 106
Assessment centres 108
Tests 115
Do your research 120
Interview skills 131
Effective speech 138
Questioning techniques 143
Listening skills 146
Non-verbal communication 151
Closing the interview 156
After the interview 156
Summary 157

Part four STEPPING BACK

Evaluating a job offer 162
Timing 168
Making the decision 169
Negotiating skills 170
Feedback 179
Keeping records 189
Summary 190

CONCLUSION

The Golden Rules 200
Useful contacts 205
Further reading 209
Index 211

INTRODUCTION

There are any number of reasons why you might have picked up this book. You may be:

- determined to find new employment and be involved in a systematic search for a new job
- seeking promotion
- considering a change in job or career
- working through the effects of downsizing or delayering in your organisation (in plain English, facing redundancy)
- returning to work after a career break
- seeking contract or freelance work through promoting your services.

Whatever your reason, this book offers useful, sensible advice on strategies that will help you move through the various stages of recruitment and selection.

How you use the book is up to you. You can read through the whole book or dip in and select the sections that are most appropriate for the task in front of you. For example, if your job search is restricted to answering press advertisements for vacancies, then you might want to read the section on sourcing job vacancies and identify new areas in which to search. If you have successfully submitted an application form or CV and been asked to attend an interview, then the sections on preparing for interview and interview skills will help you meet the selection team with confidence.

How you use the information is very much up to you. *Job Seeking* does not guarantee that you will get the job you want. What it will do is help you make the most of your skills and thus improve your chances.

Job Seeking is divided into four parts. Each part represents a series of steps you will take during your job search.

Part One: Stepping Out

The first section of Part One asks you to analyse your present position and think about why you want to change employment. It encourages you to:

- examine the reasons why you are seeking new employment
- identify what you are looking for in a new job
- analyse your professional and personal strengths.

Only by considering these issues in some detail can you decide what you are aiming to achieve and begin a constructive, systematic job search.

Assuming that you genuinely want to find a new job, Part One goes on to explore the recruitment and selection processes and suggests ways of finding vacancies. Many job seekers restrict themselves to scanning the appointments sections of the major newspapers, not realising that there are other, more focused methods of targeting potential employers.

Part Two: Stepping Forward

Having found appropriate vacancies, the next step of the job search involves making contact with recruiters. How can you make your application stand out against maybe hundreds of others? How do you prepare an appropriate CV? What contributes to a convincing covering letter? The aim of this part of the book is to improve your written communication skills so that, whatever the vacancy and method of application, you will feel confident when you submit your details. You will also look at using the telephone to establish contact with employers and work on improving your telephone skills.

Part Three: Step by Step

If you successfully negotiate the initial contact stage then you will probably be called to interview. Working on the premise that knowledge is power, Part Three looks at a range of different interview styles and processes so you can prepare for the big day.

The second section focuses on improving your interview skills. Nobody can predict what will happen in an interview but you can prepare yourself by improving both your verbal and non-verbal communication skills.

There is also advice on keeping records and monitoring your job search so that you keep track of your progress.

Part Four: Stepping Back

Part Four takes the job search through to its final stages. If you are offered a new job, how do you know it is the right one for you? Advice on evaluating job offers and negotiating reward packages will help you make a more informed and objective assessment of your options.

There is also practical information on getting and using feedback to improve your performance if your job search continues.

The Golden Rules

As you read through *Job Seeking*, you will come across The Rules. These are simple statements of good practice that any job seeker can apply to any job search.

First-hand experiences

You will find a number of anecdotes from both job seekers and recruiters. Compiled from interviews across a wide spectrum of employment disciplines, they provide a useful insight into the world of recruitment and selection. By reading these short extracts you'll pick up a lot of good advice about what to do – and what *not* to do – as your search progresses.

Exercises

This icon ✎ is used where we suggest you answer questions, make some notes or practise a task. Keep some paper by you so you can do this. Keep anything you write as you may need to refer to it later. As your job search progresses, you will compile a personal databank that covers everything from the material you include in your CV to a record of all the contacts you make and interviews you attend.

Your notes are an integral part of this databank and will help to clarify your thoughts and point you in new directions.

Part one

STEPPING OUT

GOLDEN RULE 1

Successful job seekers know why they are looking for a new job.

The days of 'a job for life' appear to be over. During a thirty-five year career span you could change jobs numerous times in a search for greater career satisfaction or because your personal or professional circumstances change. As technology impacts upon industry and commerce you may find that you need to move into a totally different career area. In other words, career change may be your choice – or it may be forced upon you.

The balance of responsibility for managing careers is shifting from organisations to individuals. Career management demands flexibility and a willingness to accept change on the part of the employee. Such change may involve seeking new employment inside or outside your current organisation.

Interviews with job seekers reveal many different reasons why they get involved in the job-seeking process.

> *'I feel I've taken this job as far as I can – I want to move to a larger organisation with more potential for advancement.'*

> *'My employers are moving to Glasgow. I either go with them or find another job. If I were on my own then I'd relocate, but I don't want to uproot my family.'*

> *'Increasingly the jobs in our sector are being taken over by systems and that's not an area I want to work in. I feel like I need to get out now before I find I don't have a job to go to.'*

'I've stayed at home to bring up my children for the past nine years. That was my decision and I was happy to do it, but now I'm ready to go back to work.'

'I love change. I get a real buzz when I start with a new company – new people, new challenges, new clients. I suppose I could work my way through the ranks with my present employer but I'm more inclined to look elsewhere after three or four years.'

'I'm a consultant working on reasonably long-term software development and implementation projects. Some contracts are won through tender, for others I canvass potential employers and go through an interview and presentation. Finding each piece of new work is a mini job-search.'

THE JOB SEEKER

As the above quotes indicate, a job search may be your choice because you:

- are looking for greater challenges
- want a better salary and benefits package
- are seeking professional development through promotion
- want a new direction in your career
- feel it is the next logical step
- are dissatisfied with the conditions and relationships in your present job
- enjoy changing jobs!

Alternatively your job search may be the result of external pressures, such as:

- redundancy

- enforced relocation
- change in job specification
- change in your personal circumstances.

To a degree, how you approach the job search will depend on the reasons you have for making a move. If the choice is yours and you do not feel that your autonomy is threatened, you will be more positive about finding new opportunities. If you feel that you have been 'pushed' into finding new employment, then your resentment may colour your attitude, making you negative towards future employers and your career prospects in general.

The unwilling job seeker

Bland and trite phrases such as 'make every setback into a new opportunity' will do little to help people who feel they are being forced into the job search. There are no easy answers to relieve your resentment, no mantra that will put you back on track. However, the hard truth is that in terms of the job search you must keep your emotions under control. A prospective new employer may secretly sympathise if you have been made redundant – but it is not their problem. They have probably, during the course of their work, made people redundant themselves. It is all part of business.

Perhaps the best advice that can be given to involuntary job seekers is to try to remain objective. Approach the job search in the same way that you would approach any business task, with thorough preparation, a plan of action and regular reviews of your progress.

As far as you can, keep your emotions out of the job-seeking arena.

Do you *really* want to move?

Before you start looking for precise information on how to improve your chances of getting the job you really want, consider your own approach to the job search. Are you seriously searching, or is looking for a new job a bit of a hobby?

> Nobody can tell you when it is the right time to change jobs; that is a decision only you can make. You can, however, weigh up the evidence in your present situation. Answer the following questions.

JOB-SEEKING QUESTIONNAIRE

Do you worry about work?	YES ☐ NO ☐
Is work adversely affecting your home life?	YES ☐ NO ☐
Is work affecting your health?	YES ☐ NO ☐
Is it more than three years since your last promotion?	YES ☐ NO ☐
Are you often bored at work?	YES ☐ NO ☐
Do you find work frustrating?	YES ☐ NO ☐
Do you sometimes feel undervalued?	YES ☐ NO ☐
Is the structure of your company changing?	YES ☐ NO ☐

Do you feel that your prospects for advancement are limited?	YES ☐	NO ☐
Do you feel nervous before going to work?	YES ☐	NO ☐
Do you often make negative comments about work?	YES ☐	NO ☐
Have you looked at job vacancies recently?	YES ☐	NO ☐

If you answered yes to six or more of these questions, your level of discontent suggests that some sort of change may be in order.

Be determined

Success in the job market demands dedication. You need to be committed to finding the job you want and willing to put aside time to support that commitment. You need to be consistent, checking your job-seeking records and making and following up opportunities every single day. You will manage the process in the same way that you would manage a project at work – systematically and thoroughly. You will regularly plan, act and review your progress.

Some lucky individuals appear to vaguely consider a move, follow up a couple of leads and fall comfortably into the ideal job. They are in the minority. For most of us, job seeking is hard work.

You may be at the stage when you are *thinking about* a move. In that case, weigh up the pros and cons and plan a course of action before you start firing off letters of application.

Think about why you are considering change, whether your present situation still holds potential and what you want to achieve. Only then will you be ready to begin your campaign.

An example

Consider Margaret's options. Margaret has worked in customer service for ten years. In recent months as the company has moved into a rapid phase of regeneration, the nature of her work has changed. She spends little time dealing directly with customers and much more time working on computerised correspondence and team projects. She finds the work rather dull, and misses the contact with customers face-to-face and on the telephone. Increasingly she feels that her highly developed interpersonal skills are no longer valued and her rather basic computer skills are inadequate for the type of work she now does. Margaret has started to look for another job.

Margaret may well find another job but she could also find that a similar situation arises in another company as the nature of customer service changes.

Before applying for another job, Margaret should consider options within her present company. She can:

- break down her responsibilities to identify exactly what she does not like
- discuss the problems with her line manager
- ask for extra training to increase her confidence in computer skills
- ask for a period in another department or function through job rotation or relocation

- consider personal development and skills-based courses that would move her in new directions.

Obviously, it is possible that none of these alternatives will solve the problem, but Margaret should not immediately rule them out. Changing jobs after ten years is a major step and one that cannot be taken lightly. It is in her interests to discuss her problems and find other possible solutions before she takes radical action.

Your situation

Before you go any further, think about your own situation.

- Ask yourself honestly why you are job seeking and make a written note of your reasons.
- What are the alternatives to moving from your present situation?
- How viable are these alternatives?
- With whom can you discuss these alternatives (your line manager, your HR manager, friends, colleagues, etc.)?

If you have explored your own options and still conclude that new employment is the answer, read the next section *before* you start looking for vacancies.

Commitment to change

'I complained to a friend that I've been looking for a new job for nearly six months

and getting nowhere. She asked how many applications I'd made during that period and when I added them up, I realised it was only about ten. That seems a lot when you are not getting anywhere but, as she pointed out, ten applications in six months is hardly making a real effort. Maybe I don't really want a new job – I just like knowing there's the potential for change.'

Job seeking is hard work. If you commit yourself to finding a new job, then you will work at it all the time. You will follow up every lead, read every piece of relevant information and constantly work to improve your communication and presentation skills. When you get back from work, you will be prepared to spend part of the evening on your job search dealing with correspondence, telephoning your network colleagues and looking for vacancies. You will not get time off for good behaviour, or because you are disheartend by a bad interview or because you want a couple of weeks' skiing in the Swiss Alps!

Are you willing to commit that much energy and time to the job search? Ask yourself the question one more time – do you really want to move to a new employer?

'When I knew that I really wanted to move on, I set myself a list of targets. They included reviewing my options and working out what I want to do next, identifying sources of new jobs and making a minimum number of approaches and applications every week. It takes time and it's hard work but at the end of every day I feel like I've done something positive.'

If you are willing to make that sort of commitment, then you are ready to start the job search.

A SYSTEMATIC APPROACH

Successful job seeking is not a random process. Taking a 'scatter gun' approach and sending off an application for any vaguely suitable vacancy takes time and energy but may gain little positive response. At some point during the recruitment and selection process, your lack of focus will show and potential employers will pick up on your lack of clear direction.

Each job application should be carefully targeted to match:

- your qualifications and experience
- your skills and competences
- your career progression.

Because every application demands research and preparation, direct your efforts towards vacancies in which you are genuinely interested. In other words, know where you are now and where you want to be, then consider every job you apply for as a vehicle for getting there.

If you are unsure about your direction or feel that your career goals need to be redefined and clarified, you may want to consult another book in the *Career PowerTools* series. *Plan Your Career* by John Lockett takes you through a number of exercises that will help you to assess your current situation and set goals for career growth. It will also help you to make key decisions about whether or not you are ready to move into new employment.

THE IDEAL JOB?

Before you make any applications, you need to sit down and think hard about what you are really looking for in a job. For many of us, career progression is something we take for granted, always looking towards the next promotion, the next pay rise, the next step up the ladder. Few people take the time to consider seriously if that is what they really want and to weigh up all the implications of a change in their employment situation. Then, when they have settled into a new job, they find themselves facing consequences they had not anticipated.

Starting a new job can be one of the most challenging and satisfying times of your career – providing that you have found the job that you want. In this section, you will consider what that job is.

Think about your career to date and then answer the questions below. They will help you to create an outline of the new job that you really want. This is not a psychometric test. It has not been developed by a psychologist to give you new insights into your own personality. What it will do is help you to clarify factors which are important in your career, such as salary, level of responsibility, the time you want to spend working, etc.

IDEAL JOB PROFILE

✎ Tick the statement (or statements, because there may be more than one) that most closely reflects your opinion. Be honest – nobody will see the answers except you.

1. Salary

Which of these is most important to you?

☐ more money immediately

☐ regular pay rises and a steadily increasing income

☐ a high disposable income

☐ a fixed salary

☐ the chance to earn money through bonuses or commission

☐ job satisfaction is a greater priority than money

Now write down the minimum salary you could afford to live on and the maximum you would hope to get.

Minimum ....

Maximum ....

2. Responsibility

Which of these is most important to you?

☐ to lead a team

☐ to be part of a team

- [ ] to make decisions and be accountable
- [ ] to have more responsibility than you do at the moment
- [ ] to have less responsibility than you do at the moment

3. Time

Which of these is most important to you?

- [ ] fixed, predictable hours
- [ ] longer holidays
- [ ] flexible working patterns
- [ ] longer hours for more money
- [ ] shorter hours for less money

4. Location

Where, ideally, would you like to work?

- [ ] close to home
- [ ] at home
- [ ] within commutable distance
- [ ] relocating is an option
- [ ] travelling overseas

5. Authority

What is your attitude to authority? Do you:

- [ ] feel comfortable taking orders?
- [ ] want control over your work?
- [ ] have a position of authority?
- [ ] want to determine the content of the work you do?

☐ want to determine the content of other people's work?

6. The organisation

Whould you prefer to work for:

☐ a small organisation?

☐ a large organisation?

☐ a respected organisation?

☐ an organisation that has high ethical standards?

☐ a successful organisation?

☐ an organisation that sets standards for the industry?

7. Opportunities

Which of the following are important to you?

☐ opportunities for regular promotion

☐ opportunities for training and development

☐ the opportunity to start new projects

☐ the opportunity to follow a project through from beginning to end

8. Work

What style of work best suits you?

☐ challenging

☐ innovative

☐ routine

☐ varied

- [ ] fast-paced
- [ ] systematic

9. Recognition

Do you want your work to be:

- [ ] recognised by your peers?
- [ ] recognised by senior management?
- [ ] recognised by other organisations?
- [ ] recognised as authoritative in your area?
- [ ] unobtrusive – you are content to work in the background?

✎ Look back over your answers and note down the most important factors that emerge. These can be put together to form a profile of your ideal job.

Of course, the chances of you finding a job that matches exactly both your preferences and your skills and aptitudes is pretty remote. Nevertheless, every time you consider a job vacancy, check it against this ideal job profile. Are there points in common? How close is the vacancy to the job you really want?

> *'For the first time in years I was really honest about what I wanted rather than considering what other people would think about me. The culture in my profession demands that you are always looking for the next stage of advancement. In fact, I was tired. I didn't want more responsibility, I didn't want more travel and I wanted to spend more time at*

home. None of which I would have dared admit in the office.'

SEEK EXPERT ADVICE

If you are really unsure about your career direction, if you feel that it is time for a career change rather than a search for a better job, then it may be worth consulting the experts. You can start by reading books on the subject, such as *Reviewing Your Career* by John Lockett. It may be worthwhile investing in careers analysis and counselling sessions. Depending on the organisation you approach, this can include working with a trained career adviser to examine your skills and aptitudes, assistance in accessing jobs, help with improving your presentation skills and analysing job offers.

If you decide to follow this course of action:

- choose a reputable organisation
- find out their fees beforehand
- check the extent of the advice you will be given.

WHAT CAN YOU OFFER?

Many companies will specify certain competences they are seeking in a new recruit. These may be occupational (job-related) competences or personal competences.

Occupational competences describe what people are expected to be able to do in a particular occupational role. They define what an employer or a particular sector of industry expects of somebody who is effective in their job. Occupational competences may be used by recruiters to describe a job precisely.

Personal competences describe key behaviours that effective job holders display when achieving the outcomes described in occupational competences. As such, they are transferable skills which can be used in any job or organisation. They can be used in recruitment and selection, to identify training needs and in staff appraisal. Personal competences cover such areas as:

- showing concern for excellence
- setting and prioritising objectives
- relating to others
- managing personal emotions and stress
- collecting and organising information
- decision making.

Organisations may define their own competences which they believe are relevant to their business. Alternatively, they may work with competence models such as those defined by the professional management bodies like the Management Charter Initiative, a government-sponsored initiative designed to improve management standards.

How do competences affect you?

If an organisation uses a competence model to recruit and select, they will define clearly the levels of skill and knowledge (both professional and personal) that they expect from the person they recruit. To find out whether candidates possess the right competences demands a more in-depth analysis during the selection process. Companies that follow this method may use assessment centres (see page 00) or simulation exercises as well as interviews to find the people they want.

One of the first steps in your job search is to identify your own job-related and personal competences so that you have a clear picture of how your profile will appear to a potential employer. In simple terms, you need to draw up a list of your skills, expertise and experience. You will use this list in your CV and at interview.

KNOW YOURSELF

Before you start asking potential employers to consider you as a member of staff, you must be clear about what you can offer them. A simple list of the jobs you have held since leaving school or university is not enough. Employers want to know what you have already achieved and what you are capable of achieving in the future. A period of self-assessment at the beginning of your job search will do much to focus your thoughts on what sort of job you are now looking for – and will make you more confident when you start making applications.

Your competence profile

✎ The headings in this checklist are derived from work on competence analysis carried out by the Harvard Business School. Look at each one. Make a brief note of how you match these criteria. It is important that you find evidence to support your claims by drawing on your past experience.

For example, under the heading 'Influence', you could cite specific examples of:

- team leadership
- projects you have managed
- mentoring.

COMPETENCE PROFILE

1. **Achievement**
   (academic, professional, personal)

2. **Effectiveness**
   (examples of effective behaviour that has impacted on your organisation)

3. **Interpersonal skills**
   (communication skills, networking, negotiating, team leadership, etc.)

4. **Persuasion**
   (examples of your ability to direct activity through persuasion)

5. **Motivation**
   (how you have motivated yourself and others to greater achievement)

6. **Flexibility**
   (how you have responded to – and implemented – change)

7. **Expertise**
   (your particular areas of expertise)

8. Influence
(what influence you have exerted on others)

9. Reasoning
(evidence of your reasoning skills related to
your work or profession)

10. Direction
(how you have directed the achievements of yourself and your colleagues)

11. Control
(examples of your authority over both your
work and that of your colleagues)

12. Business awareness
(understanding of commercial issues that impact on your area of work)

Use the information you gather under these headings as part of your personal databank. There is a section on setting this up on pages 53–55.

So far you have examined the reasons why you are seeking new employment, identified the qualities you are looking for in a new job and analysed your own professional and personal strengths.

All this information will be used in your applications, so keep any notes you have made – you will need to refer to them later.

Next, you will move on to look at the recruitment and selection processes and find out ways of sourcing new opportunities for work.

RECRUITMENT AND SELECTION

Understanding how the recruitment and selection processes work will help you exploit opportunities by knowing where employers search for new recruits and how they choose the successful applicants.

GOLDEN RULE 2

Successful job seekers gain an advantage by understanding the recruitment and selection processes.

The job market

If you have been job seeking for some time without success, you may believe that the jobs are simply not there. Research by the Department for Education and Employment indicates that you are wrong. Figures are collated every quarter to analyse labour market trends in the United Kingdom. In the first quarter of 1998, these figures suggested that:

- the economy is growing and this growth is reflected in increased levels of employment
- the number of people in employment rose by more than half a million
- unemployment is going down.

At the same time, the number of unfilled vacancies is rising and employers report difficulties in recruiting the staff they need. This is partly due to a skills shortage in certain manufacturing sectors but, interestingly, the service sector also reports recruitment difficulties.

Europe has an ageing labour market. By 2005, 80 per cent of our technology will be less than ten years old while 80 per cent of our workforce will have an education that is more than ten years old. The implication for job seekers is that they should be willing to look in new areas for employment, to think beyond their current situation and to explore new training opportunities.

The message is that the work is there, provided you know how and where to look and you remain realistic in your expectations.

It will help your job search if you understand how organisations find new staff. In the following sections you'll find out more about the recruitment and selection processes and look at various sources you can use to find job vacancies.

Obviously, not all organisations follow the same pattern. A small engineering company may not have the resources – or the inclination – to follow the sort of systematic recruitment and selection policy established by a multinational that employs thousands of people. You could find, however, that they both use similar approaches.

> *'We're a small company. When it comes to finding new staff it's basically up to me, as managing director, to oversee the whole process. I put together a job description, decide how it will be publicised and take a major role in the selection process. The final decision usually involves two or three other members of staff – line managers, colleagues who will actually work with the new member*

of staff. But in the end I suppose the decision is really mine.'

'Our Human Resources division takes care of recruitment and selection. The staff are trained in recruitment procedures and they have a systematic approach to sourcing new staff that involves carrying out a job analysis, attracting the right sort of candidates, interviewing and selecting. We've found this system works well and we have a low staff turnover. Of course, we have the necessary resources to carry out a thorough selection exercise. It might not be the same in a smaller organisation.'

RECRUITMENT

The terms 'recruitment' and 'selection' are often used synonymously. In fact, they refer to two very different processes.

Recruitment is the process of attracting suitable candidates to apply for a vacancy. The place of recruitment in many organisations has changed in recent years. Traditionally it was the responsibility of members of the personnel department who would be given details of a vacancy which they would then fill. Now it is more of a strategic activity, involving members of the organisation at all levels. For example, a human resource management policy may be formulated by directors as part of their overall plan for the organisation's development; line managers may be asked to contribute to job descriptions;

selection interviews may involve a range of people from senior management through to junior support staff.

The recruitment process involves analysing a job, developing a profile of the type of person who will most likely succeed in that job and finding the right places in which to publicise the vacancy.

To carry out these tasks effectively, the recruiter needs to understand the organisation's requirements, to develop an understanding of specific jobs and functions and to have a broad knowledge of the employment marketplace. Specifically:

- What skills does the job demand?
- What experience does the job demand?
- What skills and competences are required?
- Where are suitable candidates most likely to be found?
- What is the level of demand for people who might fill this vacancy?
- What sort of package will a new recruit anticipate?

At the recruitment stage, the recruiter will:

- carry out a job analysis
- develop a job description
- develop a person specification
- search for candidates.

A job analysis involves finding out information about the job so that people (such as recruiters and managers who don't actually do the work) understand fully what tasks are carried out. From this information, the recruiter develops a job description and specifies the type of person who will be the 'best fit' for the post.

The job description states:

- the job title and name of the function or department in which it is carried out
- an outline of the job with a list of main tasks
- a description of the job content which analyses these tasks in some detail. The main elements are a description of what is done, how it is done, why it is done, the anticipated standards of performance or targets and the working conditions. Obviously, it is much easier to write this section for manual or technical jobs than for managerial ones where tasks may be less precise.

A person specification contains three elements:

- intellectual requirements, such as academic and professional qualifications and skills
- physical requirements, if these apply
- personality requirements – the way in which someone interacts with others and the behaviours that are expected by the organisation. Of the three elements, this is the most difficult to quantify.

All this information must be distilled into manageable formats such as job and person specifications that are included in a careers information pack. Alternatively, they may form the basis of an advertisement which appears in the press.

The next step is to find the most appropriate method of searching for candidates by advertising the vacancy or consulting recruitment professionals.

SELECTION

Once a sufficient number of candidates have shown an interest in the job, the selection process gets under way.

During selection, candidates are assessed in order to find the right person to fill the vacancy. Anyone involved in the selection process needs a knowledge of interview techniques and selection tests, and a clear understanding of what the organisation is looking for in a new recruit.

In the early stages, particularly if there is a high volume of applicants for a post or the organisation has a very systematised approach to selection, application forms or CVs may be scored against a template. Points will be given for a range of categories such as education, background, relevant training, experience and specified skills and competences. This process is designed to get rid of unsuitable applicants as quickly as possible. That doesn't mean that, as a job seeker, if you don't have all the qualities listed in a job specification or advertisement you should not apply. If you believe your qualities match 70 per cent or more of those the employer specifies, it is worth putting in an application.

Recruitment and selection may not be carried out by the same person in the organisation. Some companies will use an outside agency to preselect and to compile a short list of candidates who will be interviewed. Alternatively, preselection may be carried out by members of the human resources team, while the final selection is the responsibility of functional managers or directors.

Almost all organisations use some form of interview during the selection process. This may involve a single meeting or an assessment centre (see page 108). The short-listed candidates will be brought together for an interview with key personnel. Finally, the candidate who best meets the organisation's needs as defined in the job and person specifications will be selected and offered the job.

Human resource planning
to identify what the organisation needs

↓

Job analysis sets out what the job
involves and the type of applicant required

↓

Recruitment strategy is identified
to attract suitable candidates

↓

Preselection

↓

Short-listed candidates invited
for interview

↓

Selection to find the most suitable
candidate

A typical recruitment process

SEARCHING FOR THE RIGHT CANDIDATE

> **GOLDEN RULE 3**
>
> Successful job seekers know where to look for suitable vacancies.

From the employer's point of view, finding the right candidate for the job is essential. The quality of staff affects the success of the organisation in terms of profitability, image and future development. Failure to recruit and select successfully can be very expensive, particularly if someone takes a job, proves unsuitable and then leaves. Research for Investors in People in April 1998 (quoted in the *Independent*, 5 April 1998) suggests that replacing a member of staff can cost up to £15,000. Recruiting unsuitable staff who *don't* leave can also cause problems, leading to inefficiency, problems with other employee relations and a high staff turnover.

Employers recruit from either inside the organisation (internal recruitment) or from outside (external recruitment). There are pros and cons for both options. The approach an organisation chooses depends on a variety of factors such as cost, the urgency with which they need to fill a vacancy and the success of recruitment methods they have used in the past. It is also worth noting that organisations often use different recruitment methods to fill vacancies at different levels. For example, they may use an executive search agency for senior or professional posts, advertise in the press for middle managers, and contact local Jobcentres to fill support grades from the local population.

Internal recruitment

This can be achieved by:

- promotion from within
- job rotation where staff are temporarily redeployed to other jobs
- re-hiring employees who have been made redundant
- advertising jobs internally.

For the employer, it is a cheap option for finding new recruits and has the advantage of keeping recruitment 'in the family'. Employees moving into new jobs will already be familiar with the organisation's culture and practices, and that can save a lot of time in getting a new post up and running. For employees, it can also be a bonus to work for a company that recruits internally, since theoretically there will be greater opportunities for mobility and promotion.

There are drawbacks, however. Staff may become very political to gain advancement and this can disrupt teams and departments. If staff are regularly transferred from one division to another, some areas may well become understaffed if there is a lack of suitable applicants from within the company. Finally, and perhaps most crucially, internal recruitment does not allow for 'new blood' to be injected into the organisation, bringing fresh perspectives and ideas.

As a job seeker, don't rule out internal recruitment. Within flatter organisational structures, moving sideways can be an ideal way to learn new skills and change your career path. Earlier in Part One you were asked to assess your present situation. One question to address is whether you could find the job you want within your own organisation. If so, then check internal vacancy listings, and talk to your line manager and your human resources manager.

External recruitment

Recruiting from outside the organisation offers access to a wide pool of applicants and brings in 'new blood'. On the other hand, it can be costly, slow and the results may not be totally successful since neither the candidate nor the organisation may have a true picture of each other after the relatively short selection process.

External recruitment takes place through a variety of sources, all of which you should consider as you search for appropriate vacancies.

Employment agencies

These are particularly useful if the employer is looking for specialists, has regular vacancies to fill (such as seasonal vacancies), or needs a high volume of recruits. They also provide a valuable service to employers who do not have the trained personnel, time or inclination to carry out the recruitment and selection processes themselves. Agencies can provide preselection or selection services and they should be able to draw on a fairly wide database of interested and qualified applicants.

Executive search

Variously known as headhunters, search and selection, etc., these companies access applicants who are not actively looking for a new job but who would consider a move if the right vacancy was presented to them. Usually such agencies specialise in a particular area and work on a fairly senior level, seeking out senior managers and professional staff for employers. This can be an expensive way of recruiting since executive search consultancies can charge fees of up to one-third of the first year's salary of a new employee.

Outplacement consultancy

This is a newer type of employment agency which specialises in finding jobs for people who are about to be made redundant, rather than finding people to fill vacancies. Employers may find themselves approached by outplacement consultancies with details of individuals who would be suitable for specific functions in their organisations.

Advertisements

Probably the first point of reference for the majority of job seekers, advertising is not generally considered by employers to be the most effective method of finding the right recruits. It can be expensive and, if advertisements are not carefully structured and targeted, can lead to a deluge of unsuitable applications which then have to be processed.

This is the 'visible job market'. The advertisements you see every day in the newspapers, every week in professional journals or advertised on the Internet are open to anybody who reads them. They are easy to find and consequently attract the most applicants. Although advertisements may be the most obvious place to start looking for a new job, they are the medium through which you face the most competition. Your chances of receiving a positive reply (or any reply at all) are low compared to applications you make through alternative sources.

If you are checking newspaper advertisements as a means of finding a new job, you should be aware of how the system works. Employers can contact specialist agencies to develop advertisements and advertise in the right newspapers. These agencies know which newspapers will provide the most suitable candidates for particular types of vacancy. For example, the *Guardian* regularly fields a high volume of media and public sector jobs, presumably because advertisers believe that the type of employee they are seeking is more likely to be found browsing the pages of the *Guardian* than the *Daily Telegraph*.

Professional journals have a more specialised audience. This gives employers a tighter focus and ensures their advertisement reaches an appropriately qualified and skilled audience. For the job seeker, this more limited audience is a bonus since it reduces the level of competition in terms of numbers – but of course the quality of the competition may be fierce.

Because so many people follow up advertisements, applications demand particular care and attention. Your CV or application form must stand out from the rest and your approach must be strong enough to attract attention. Read Part Two to find out more about making the first written approach to a potential new employer.

Networking

Many employers recruit staff through their own network of contacts because it is a cheap, fast method of finding new people. By spreading information about vacancies to existing staff, they can encourage applications from their employees' family, friends and acquaintances.

For the job seeker, finding job opportunities through personal contacts is, statistically, the most successful route to employment. You are not in direct competition with large numbers of other applicants. You may also find that your name has been passed informally to very high levels within the organisation.

To network successfully you must be prepared to let it be known that you are in the job market. Secondly, you have to be willing to talk to people. Friends, acquaintances, former employers, professional advisers, fellow members of your Sunday soccer team, other mothers at the ante-natal class, people you know well and people you scarcely know at all – be prepared to bring your job search to their attention.

The wider you throw your net, the more opportunities you will find. After all, people know people who know people – and somebody out there will know of possible vacancies.

You may be a natural networker who sees it as a normal function of everyday life. Alternatively, the idea of networking may seem like a form of exploitation and you could be uncomfortable with the idea of 'using' people to help you find a job. Don't be. Whether you realise it or not, you are already networking all the time.

- A friend asks you where she can find a decent hairdresser and you refer her to your own salon – you are networking.
- You recommend your insurance agent to a colleague – you are networking.
- You ask a friend at the rugby club if their organisation is recruiting sales managers – you are networking.

Networking succeeds because people want to help. If somebody comes to you with a request for information or asks you directly to help, what is your usual reaction? Do you tell them to go away and bother somebody else, or do you make some effort to give them the information they need? For most of us, it is the latter. When somebody asks us for help and we are in a position to give it, we feel powerful. It's as simple as that. Networking improves our self-image.

So, when you are using your network to help in your job search, remember that you are giving others a chance to help you, giving them an opportunity to feel the power of giving. That puts a completely different perspective on asking for information or assistance!

You can take a more detailed look at successful networking by reading another book in the *Career PowerTools* series, *Powerful Networking* by John Lockett.

Direct approaches

Making a direct approach involves targeting organisations for which you want to work. It demands a great deal of preparation before you get to the point of sending in your CV. Researching the market for organisations that actually use your skills saves you a lot of time and effort. If you send out your details at random to any company that catches your eye, you can anticipate a low response rate.

This is perhaps the most difficult way to find vacancies, but with careful targeting it can be one of the most successful. You can select companies on the basis of information you receive through your network; friends and acquaintances may tell you of suitable employers who are looking for staff. Alternatively you might target companies because you know you have the relevant experience to offer them services they need.

If, for example, you work in direct marketing, you can find the names of companies in this field through Yellow Pages, or Yellow Pages on the Internet. The latter is particularly useful if you are looking for organisations outside your local area since it allows you to search across the country (indeed, around the world) for the type of company you want. Before you start firing off your details to all these companies, do some research. Some of them may be little more than the proverbial 'man and his dog'. Ring up and ask for details of the company; say that you are looking into recruitment in that particular area. If the company can send you information about its work, request it. Find out the name of the person in charge of human resources or, in a smaller company, the managing director. You then have a named contact to send your details to at a later date.

When making a direct approach, send a copy of your CV and a carefully worded covering letter (there is more about covering letters in Part Two). In letters for this particular type of approach it is important not only to state clearly why you are writing but also to make it clear that you are not automatically expecting a job offer. You are making a first approach, making contact on which you can build later. If you don't put the employer in the embarrassing position of feeling that you expect something from them, you stand a better chance of developing an ongoing dialogue that puts you in prime position should a suitable vacancy arise later.

On-line recruitment

The Internet is the job advertisement medium of the nineties. Hundreds of thousands of jobs around the world are advertised every day on the Internet. Thousands of these are British vacancies so, as a possible source of contacts for job seekers, it has to be explored. Companies may choose to advertise through their own Web sites or through commercial job sites such as Guardian Recruitnet.

Because computer screens offer more space than conventional printed advertisements, you may find more detailed job specifications which offer better guidance on what employers are looking for – and what they are offering.

Not surprisingly, at the moment many of the Internet sites dedicated to job seeking are for computer-related jobs, particularly contract work. There are, however, more generalist sites which help you access vacancies by profession. For example, Guardian Recruitnet, posted by the *Guardian* newspaper, helps you find appropriate job opportunities by selecting your particular industry or professional area, the location in which you want to work and the salary to which you aspire. It then trawls through all available vacancies, and selects those which most closely match your specification. For each vacancy you have the option of looking at a second screen which offers a more detailed job specification. The system is quick, easy to use and you can access it 24 hours a day.

Many dedicated job sites also offer job-seeking advice and information. Even more useful, there are sites that allow you to 'post' your own CV on the Internet where it will be seen by recruitment agencies and employers who are looking for staff. You will be offered a standard form to complete with your personal and professional details. No technical expertise is necessary unless you aspire to creating your own pages on the Internet.

Theoretically, job hunting on-line saves you a lot of trouble. No more ploughing through newspaper appointment sections, no more time-consuming appointments with recruitment consultants. You do need to be aware of some drawbacks, however. Not all employers want to work on-line and some will continue to use more conventional recruitment methods, such as advertising in the press or contacting recruitment agencies. Then there is the problem of information overload. There are thousands of vacancies on the Internet; there is also an increasing number of job seekers using its service, with thousands of CVs being posted every day. Lastly, it is worth remembering that the Internet can be used and accessed by anybody who has a computer and modem. Not all individuals and organisations are quite what they seem.

It is doubtful that you will be offered a job solely through an Internet advertisement and application – indeed, you should be suspicious if you are. As with the standard postal approach, your CV will be the initial method of contact and you should expect an interview if an employer is genuinely interested in your application. For your own safety, check out any employer who contacts you via the Internet before you arrange to meet them. Ring Directory Enquiries, give the name and address and ask for confirmation of the company's telephone number. Alternatively, check business directories to make sure the company actually exists.

Internet job sites change rapidly so it would be pointless to include a list here. There are sites attached to many of the national newspapers and to recruitment consultancies such as Reed International. Web site addresses occasionally appear in the press – or you could search the Internet using key words such as 'job seeking' and 'recruitment'.

> 'Using the Internet has revolutionised my ideas about looking for a job. I can log on at any time, establish specialist searches, even have suitable vacancies posted to my e-mail address as soon as they appear. I'm also using it to find out more about companies that work in my area and to research organisations that I approach for an

interview. The great thing is that I can do all of this when I want – at midnight or seven o'clock in the morning. I'm no longer reliant on newspapers, libraries and other people's business hours.'

....

SUMMARY

You have now spent some time thinking about what you really want from a new job, explored the recruitment and selection processes and looked at different methods you can use to identify vacancies.

As a systematic job seeker, you will use this information to prepare yourself for the next stage in your job search – contacting potential employers.

Part Two of *Job Seeking* is entitled 'Stepping Forward'. The title reflects what you will do next – step forward and make yourself known through answering advertisements and making speculative approaches.

Part two
STEPPING FORWARD

In Part one you looked at possible sources of new jobs and began to identify where you will find vacancies.

The next step is to make the first approach to a potential employer. There are many ways of making that first approach, including:

- preparing a CV and covering letter in reply to an advertisement
- completing an application form
- making telephone contact with a preselector
- an informal meeting or telephone call in response to an approach from a network contact or search consultant.

How you make that first approach depends on where you locate the vacancy. There is no standard approach; you cannot prepare a single CV and covering letter, store it on your computer, print it and send it out each time you come across a new job opportunity. Each vacancy demands an individual approach and it is up to you to choose the most appropriate style for your application.

Recruitment and selection can be very subjective. Yes, many large organisations have carefully structured systems designed to take a systematic approach to recruitment and selection. Theoretically, this removes any element of personal bias. But you may be applying for a job with an organisation where tasks are carried out on a more ad hoc basis. Recruitment and selection may be the remit of a dedicated human resources function within the company, or they may be processes the managing director prefers to supervise personally.

You could apply to a company which expects a strongly worded, functional CV. Equally, you may apply to a firm where a more traditional approach is required or one where proactive, informal 'in your face' tactics gain you an advantage.

There are no certainties. You can, however, research the prospective employer to get some idea of their management style to help you decide how to make your approach. You can gather information about the job itself and the type of person they are looking for. Use this information to tailor your application to meet the employer's needs.

Part Two of *Job Seeking* looks at skills and tactics you will use to make the initial approach to a prospective new employer. It helps you:

- prepare a personal databank
- interpret advertisements
- improve your written and verbal communication skills
- polish your telephone technique
- prepare your CV
- complete application forms
- prepare different styles of covering letter.

YOUR PERSONAL DATABANK

The basis of any application will be your personal databank. Stored either on a PC or on reference cards, this is an up-to-date record of all your achievements.

If you think that preparing and maintaining the databank is a waste of time because you can remember all you've done, either you have an excellent memory, or you have led a very sheltered life. Either way, you will be in danger of overlooking vital experience that could help your job applications.

The purpose of the databank is to record achievements, however small, that could be relevant to a prospective employer. This involves a lot of detail that you are unlikely simply to remember and recall when you need it. Consequently it makes sense to keep an *aide memoire* readily to hand.

You will use only a small percentage of this information when you prepare your CV or complete an application form. The rest of the information will prove useful in interviews as a stimulus for discussion; you will also find it encouraging to sit back occasionally and review the extent of your own experience.

Preparing your personal databank

✎ Use the following headings to compile a personal databank. First, go back to the list you compiled in Part One of your professional and personal competences (p. 28–29). Include that information where it is relevant under the headings. Pay attention to detail (such as checking dates, names and addresses) during the initial stages because this will save you time later when you are preparing applications.

OUTLINE OF PERSONAL DATABANK

1. **Education**
   (names of schools and colleges, dates attended, exams and grades)

2. **Professional qualifications**
   (names of awarding bodies, dates, grades consistent with (1) above)

3. **Work experience**
   (reverse chronological order, names and addresses of employers, dates, job titles)

4. **Professional achievements**
   (any particular projects you have worked on, publications, etc.)

5. **Job-related competences**
   (refer to the list you made when reading Part One)

6. **Personal competences**
   (refer to the list you made when reading Part One)

7. **Day-to-day responsibilities**
   (for example, tasks involving leadership and teamworking skills, information analysis, decision making, etc.)

8. **Special responsibilities**
   (for example, tasks which have been delegated specifically to you)

9. **Learning, training and development activities**
   (include formal courses, on-the-job training, temporary promotion, job rotation, secondments, work shadowing, etc., with dates)

10 **Extra curricular achievements**
   (for example, voluntary work, sports, membership of non-professional organisations)

Using your databank

Successful job applications are closely targeted to the employer's specifications. It's all about giving the employer what he or she wants. Use your personal databank to help you compile an application that relates clearly to the specifications of the vacancy.

On a more mundane level, the databank will help you to pull together factual information such as the dates of your education and different jobs – a task that becomes more difficult as your career progresses and your experience mounts up!

Check your databank regularly and add to it every time your responsibilities and experience change.

....

INTERPRETING THE ADVERTISEMENT

| GOLDEN RULE 4 |

Successful job seekers tailor every approach to meet the needs of the employer.

Some advertisements are absolutely precise about what qualifications and experience an employer requires, others are more vague. Some advertisements are works of art in terms of concept and copywriting but tell you almost nothing about the vacancy.

Look at the examples in the three figures below.

Planning and Compliance Manager

You will lead a team that creates standards for operation of the data network. Responsibilities include: IT security, capacity planning, change control administration, software product testing and acceptance procedures, contingency planning and performance monitoring.

Essential skills and experience:

- 5+ years experience in a similar position
- staff management experience
- experience of operating within an ISO 9000 compliant system

---

A precisely worded advertisement

Senior Lecturer Curriculum Development

Educated to a minimum of Master's degree level, the successful applicant will have excellent writing skills and a sound knowledge of ENB standards ... He/she will be committed to multi-professional education. An active interest in education research would be an advantage.

Personality wanted – with copy writing skills

Do you live and breath superb copy? Are you hungry to work for an innovative, dynamic company at the forefront of change … ?

We're looking for someone who's:

- as ambitious as we are, bursting with energy and really up for it
- a perfectionist – prepared to nail every sentence, every word, every comma
- able to manage their time well, prioritise work and put in the hours where necessary
- got a feel about the way we like to communicate with our customers
- able to write about financial products in a way that brings them to life.

A creative advertisement

As you read advertisements, you will be able to weed out those:

- that don't interest you
- for which you are not qualified
- for which you lack the necessary experience.

That should leave you with a number of 'possible' vacancies. You can apply for these and stand a good chance of getting to the next stage of recruitment.

What if you are looking in a specialist area or feel that the majority of vacancies are not available to you because you lack some of the specified background? The general rule of thumb is that if you match the specification by 70 per cent or more, then it is worth applying. Areas where employers may be willing to compromise include years of experience and age. Less easy to negotiate are professional or technical qualifications and essential experience, particularly at middle management level and above.

Age should not be a problem, but unfortunately in certain areas ageism is present and overtly stated in recruitment literature that specifies applicants should be '25 to 30'. Companies practise such policies for a number of reasons: they may be hooked on presenting a young image; they may feel that they operate in an industry that demands a youthful approach; they may simply pay badly and know that older applicants with good experience would laugh at the salaries they offer. Whatever the reason, until the government puts ageism on a par with sexism and racism, it remains an obstacle mature job seekers face in some industries.

If you see a vacancy that you know you could fill but it specifies an age range in which you do not fit, apply for it anyway. Highlight your relevant experience, particularly any recent training that shows you are aware of current trends in your profession. Your experience and expertise should speak for themselves and make you worth interviewing. Any employer worth working for will accept this. If they don't, if age is such an issue to them, do you really want to work for them?

RESPONDING TO ADVERTISEMENTS

Follow the instructions in the advertisement. You may be asked to:

- submit a CV and covering letter
- telephone for an application pack
- telephone for a 'chat' – that usually means a preliminary telephone interview.

If the organisation gives a telephone number then use it. You can even risk finding out the telephone number if it is not given and making a call. A preliminary telephone conversation can help you to target your application covering letter more clearly. At best, you will be able to get through to someone connected with the recruitment process and discuss the vacancy with them. Get their name – you may need to contact them again. At the very least, you can get the name of the person you should send your details to and thus avoid the perils of addressing the female human resources manager as 'Dear Sir'.

Should you strike lucky and get through to somebody who is willing to talk, try to find out:

- more about the company and where you can get information
- details of the recruitment procedure, particularly the type of interview and the timescale for selection
- some idea of how many applications they have received.

After you have submitted your application, wait a couple of days and then call again to check it has been received. Handled diplomatically, you are showing enthusiasm and creditable initiative rather than being a nuisance. You will also put your own mind at rest if you don't hear anything for a while by knowing that the application is in the right hands.

IMPROVING YOUR WRITTEN COMMUNICATION SKILLS

GOLDEN RULE 5

Successful job seekers spend time on correspondence.

Your initial letter, CV or completed application form are the first point of contact between you and an employer. These pieces of paper can make the difference between you getting an interview (and thus a real opportunity to get the job you want) and finding your skills, talents and expertise filed in the bin.

> 'Recently I advertised in the national press for a new account manager. I expected a healthy response – we were offering a challenging job with an excellent benefits package. What I didn't anticipate were the sackfuls of mail that started to arrive on my desk two days after the advertisement appeared. I thought I'd written precise job and person specifications but obviously the criteria weren't stringent enough! In total I had more than 450 responses.

> 'Working through them was a nightmare and I have to admit my initial selection criteria were pretty arbitrary. I filed any envelope with a second class stamp straight in the bin without opening it – if they didn't think we were worth first-class post, they were not our sort of applicant. Then I ditched any CVs printed on coloured paper or badly laid out, and any with a typed covering letter because we had specified that it should be handwritten. Amazingly I got rid of more than 60 replies straight away. Maybe it's not the most scientific way of preselecting, but I had to start somewhere.'

The amount of time you spend writing reports, letters, research papers, memos, faxes and e-mails in your working life is irrelevant when it comes to job seeking. Writing a successful job application employs precise skills.

General tips for all correspondence

There is detailed advice on preparing a CV, writing a covering letter and completing application forms later in this section. But first, here are some general tips that apply to all correspondence.

1. Plan what you want to say before you write

Sketch out your ideas in note form, refine them, cut out irrelevancies – *then* start writing. This is the only way you can ensure that your letters say what you want them to say and don't wander off the point.

2. Draft and redraft

Notes → first draft → second draft → finished result. It may seem a cumbersome and lengthy process to write a letter or complete an application form, but it gives you the chance to spot shortcomings in your correspondence, to improve the fluency of your sentences and to prepare a really polished final version.

3. Stretch your word power

With hundreds of thousands of words to choose from, the English language surely offers some that are appropriate to you. Use a dictionary and thesaurus to extend your vocabulary and liven up your written communications. Learn to be positive when you talk about yourself by using 'action words' and avoiding bland, meaningless words and phrases such as 'it has been a good experience'. Resist the temptation to go overboard, however. 'Such a positive and life-enhancing project has ameliorated my expertise' is not likely to impress anybody.

4. Check and check again

Any correspondence you send out, whether it is a letter, application form or CV, needs to be proofread. Ask a friend or partner to check it for you; fresh eyes are likely to spot mistakes that you have missed.

Avoid relying on the spelling and grammar checking functions in computer software packages. These are useful to carry out a first check for faulty spelling or grammar, but they only recognise the errors for which they have been programmed. For example, they might tell you to check if you have used 'their' or 'there' correctly – but they won't tell you which is the correct version for that particular sentence. They may prevent a double word error, but they will not enhance your fluency.

5. Be brief

Say what you need to say and then stop. Think about that human resource manager wading through the 450 applications for one post. She needs a summary of what you have to offer, not your autobiography. Aim for short sentences, concise paragraphs, one-page letters and two-page CVs.

6. Take care with presentation

Take a final look at your letter, CV or application form before you put it in the envelope. Would you want to know more about the person who sent it? If you can honestly answer yes, then there is a strong chance the person who receives it will feel the same way.

Presentation is important. Layout, the use of appropriate font sizes and typefaces, even the quality of the stationery can influence the response of the person who opens the envelope. There is plenty of received wisdom on how to create an eye-catching piece of correspondence, but research with selectors suggests that the traditional approach still holds the advantage. Use good quality (100 gsm) white paper, keep the appearance clean and spacious, and avoid gimmicks such as fancy typefaces. Times Roman 12-point is easy to read and creates a professional finish.

7. Look at your language

In all correspondence, your aim is to communicate your message clearly and in a manner which captures the attention of the reader. You will do this more effectively if you use language with which you feel at ease. Stilted or complex sentences, archaic vocabulary and overemphasis produce dull, worthy but pompous prose.

8. Use plain English

Keep your language and phrasing straightforward. Conventions in writing are changing; it is both acceptable and desirable to write in the same way that you speak – using plain English.

Look at this example:

> *I hope that you will consider my application favourably and look forward to hearing from you at your earliest convenience.*

Although the sentiments are straightforward, the syntax is too complicated and the overall effect is stilted. What is the writer trying to say? The first half of the sentence is unnecessary – if she did not want her application to be considered favourably then she would not be sending it in. The second half of the sentence is a stock phrase inviting a response. It would be sufficient to say:

> *I look forward to hearing from you.*

9. Avoid redundant words

If preparing written documents is a major part of your work, you will be used to editing text to make sure it is succinct and to the point. Editing tidies up prose and also helps to tighten it up by removing redundant phrases and substituting more expressive or relevant words.

Look at this example:

In reply to the advertisement for a regional sales manager which you placed in The Times *on 26 July, 1998, I have great pleasure in enclosing a copy of my CV in support of my application.*

The wording is clumsy and verbose. Far simpler to highlight the advertisement as a heading to the letter and concentrate on what you really want to say.

Regional Sales Manager:* The Times, *26 July 1998
In response to your advertisement, I enclose my CV. I have both the qualifications and experience you require ...

10. Use the active voice

Active verbs give power and immediacy to your writing.
 Instead of stating:

A suggestion was made by the Board that I lead the department ... (passive)

say

The Board suggested that I lead the department ... (active)

11. Use action verbs

As well as using the active rather than passive voice, find action verbs to describe what you do. The aim is to sound positive, dynamic and in control; you can use language to achieve that aim. Examples of action verbs that might describe your responsibilities include:

administer	*facilitate*
analyse	*manage*
co-ordinate	*supervise*
design	*implement*
develop	*generate*
initiate	*determine*
lead	*authorise*
organise	*initiate*

12. Avoid sexism

You can very easily avoid overt sexism in language – and it is advisable to do so.
Use:

executive	instead of	*businessman*
supervisor	instead of	*foreman*
you/person	instead of	*man*
manager	instead of	*manageress*

We have already suggested that you avoid using the bland 'Dear Sir or Madam'. Rather than sending an application to an unnamed 'Managing Director' or 'Human Resources Manager', ring the company first and establish the name of the person to whom you should write.

13. Understand the conventions

Despite modernisation of many conventions, such as the removal of indents from the beginning of paragraphs and the absence of punctuation in addresses, certain formulas in correspondence remain:

- a letter which begins 'Dear Sir' should end with 'Yours faithfully' – although you are not going to use 'Dear Sir', are you?
- a letter which begins 'Dear [*followed by a name*]' should end 'Yours sincerely'
- dates should be standardised, e.g. 5 June 1999.

Now that you have looked at advice that applies to all correspondence, you can move on to create one of your most powerful job-seeking tools, your CV.

PREPARING THE RIGHT CV

| GOLDEN RULE 6 |

Successful job seekers have more than one CV.

There is no such thing as the single, perfect CV. There are plenty of books on the market that will advise you on creating a good CV, but they generally reflect the preferences and experience of the author. What you will find in *Job Seeking* is advice on a number of different styles of CV, together with guidance on how to select the right format for each application. Remember that individual approach to each job vacancy? This is where you put it into action. Every time you apply for a vacancy, ask yourself how you should adjust your CV to meet the needs of a specific job.

Think of your CV as your personal advertisement or marketing literature. Read it through and ask yourself: 'Does this person impress me? Would I like to meet them?'

Most selectors are looking for the answers to a number of questions when they read a CV, namely:

- Who is this person?
- Can they do the job?
- Will they fit in with the organisation?

Your task is to identify the information they are asking for and to present that information in a way that catches the selector's eye.

Layout

Plan and prepare your CV so that it looks attractive:

- use space to break up the text
- avoid complicated fonts, tricksy typefaces and fancy trimmings such as shaded boxes and Gothic headings
- aim for a totally professional finish by using good quality white paper and a clear printer.

Style

Write in the first person. A surprising number of people write about themselves as 'he' or 'she', presumably to avoid sounding egocentric by continually saying 'I'. If, as a matter of habit, you talk about yourself in the third person, then there might be some excuse, but otherwise all you produce is a CV that looks contrived.

Depending on the amount of work experience you have and the type of job for which you are applying, you may choose to prepare a chronological, functional or experience-based CV. We will look at all three styles soon.

Length

Your CV should be no more than two pages long. Any more and you are probably including irrelevant information – and your reader will switch off. Plus, a brief CV shows an ability to address a task precisely, to summarise information efficiently and to stick to the point – all valuable skills that you will need in your job.

Within academic circles, however, your CV should include research and publications and therefore may be longer than two pages.

Focus

Everything in your CV should be relevant to the job you are applying for. Yes, it may be interesting that three years ago you published a best-selling novel, but is this relevant to your application for the post of petrochemical engineer? By all means keep these interesting facts about yourself in mind and use them when and where you can to give a more extensive picture of yourself. But don't expect to include everything you have achieved in the last ten or fifteen years in your CV.

Chronological, functional or experience based?

During the early years of your career when you

may have a wealth of qualifications but little experience, the chronological CV will best serve your needs. It gives a clear outline of who you are, your academic and professional achievements and a brief summary of your career to date.

As your career progresses, your skills base and experience will increase. These may be the aspects on which you want to focus, rather than the subject of your dissertation for your degree course. In this case, a functional CV will focus attention on the qualities that make you the right recruit for a job.

Alternatively, the vacancy may ask for information that indicates experience in a particular field. For such a vacancy, you should consider preparing a CV that is based around your employment history and flags up your relevant work experience.

These are recommendations rather than hard and fast rules. Many selectors have their own preferences and there is no way that you can predict these. However, bear in mind the comment of one human resources manager:

> *'I'm more likely to focus on a CV that closely matches the job and person specification I have already prepared. Time is paramount when we are recruiting. I don't have days to wade through CVs looking for relevant experience and skills. I expect the applicant to have done that part of the work for me by laying out clearly how they meet the demands of the job.'*

Chronological CV

The chronological CV outlines your qualifications and experience in date (or reverse date) order. It has a number of advantages:

- it is easy to follow
- it traces the development of your career
- it summarises key achievements
- it is (or should be) precise and information based.

There are drawbacks, though:

- it may not offer sufficient space for you to list key skills
- it allows less scope for your personality to emerge
- it is harder to match this type of CV to a job specification.

Typically, a chronological CV will contain a number of sections:

1. Essential data

Name, address, telephone and fax numbers, e-mail address.

2. Profile

These are the three or four lines that briefly sum up who you are and what you do. Preparing this takes practice. Think about how you introduce yourself to new people.

> *My name is Jane Smith, I'm a retail sales manager and for the last six years I've been working for ABC Clothing.*

Now translate this into a written description. Add information that is directly relevant to the job you are applying for and highlight ways in which you can do the job – but don't turn this section into a detailed exposition of your talents. That can come later. For example:

> *A graduate in Business Studies, I have worked*

in retail for the past ten years. I manage a branch of ABC Clothing, a women's fashion outlet in London, and take overall responsibility for the running of the store and its team of six staff.

3. Educational history

If you are just starting your career, you can begin this section with a brief account of your secondary education qualifications. List your A levels, starting with the highest grade first.

Otherwise, begin with college or university. Include any professional qualifications gained from educational establishments but not in-house training qualifications.

List your educational history in chronological order and include:

- dates attended
- name of institution
- subject
- result.

4. Employment history

Set this out in reverse chronological order, starting with your present or most recent job. Avoid leaving unexplained gaps; if you do, be prepared to account for them at interview.

Include:

- dates of employment
- employer's name and location
- type of business
- your job title.

Whether you include a summary of your main responsibilities at this point is really a question of space and layout. By all means put them in here providing it doesn't make the document look cluttered. Alternatively, add a separate section to outline your responsibilities and achievements. List them under headings or in a couple of paragraphs.

Think of this part of your CV as 'added value'. What can you include that illustrates your particular strengths? If you are just starting your career, you may want to include:

- work placements
- voluntary work
- positions of responsibility in groups or associations
- travel.

The more you can put in here the better – it gives the selector an opportunity to get a broader picture of you as a person. Don't undersell yourself; equally, avoid making claims you cannot substantiate.

5. Publications

Include any relevant publications at this point. This will include the title of your dissertation or thesis and any professional articles you have published.

6. Personal details

Remember that you are under no obligation to include details of your marital status, number of children, age or nationality unless they are relevant to the job, so the choice of how much you include is yours.

If you do want to include such information, think about where to place it. Some CVs include personal details at the beginning, but there is a good reason why placing them at the end is a better idea. Hopefully by focusing on your experience, career history and qualifications, you will gain the selector's interest. It is on these factors that you want them to judge you rather than your age or the state of your driving licence.

Include:

- date of birth
- nationality
- marital status (optional)
- skills such as driving licence, languages, computer literary, etc.

Membership of a professional organisation suggests that you take your work seriously. You may also want to include your hobbies and interests, but that is really a matter of taste. Do you have some extra-curricular interests that reflect well on your abilities? For example, chairperson of a sports club indicates a degree of organisation and commitment – although the reaction to your interests may vary. It may be wise to keep quiet if you spend your weekends doing dangerous sports like sky diving. Some companies may not favour their staff risking life and limb for fun!

If you choose to include referees at the end of your CV, clear it with them first. Referees may comment on your personal qualities such as your reliability, attitude towards responsibility and motivation, or they may refer specifically to your performance at work. Choose referees who know you fairly well and who are willing to take the time to support your job applications. Increasingly, referees are approached by telephone and it helps if they know when to expect calls from selectors. If you do give details of referees, include:

- names of two different people
- their relationship to you
- title or academic title if appropriate
- contact address
- telephone number.

Functional CVs

The advantage of the functional CV is that it lets you organise your own skills and experience to match the requirements of the job. So, before you start make sure you have a copy of the job advertisement or specification to hand.

The functional CV can follow a number of formats, but the most clear is:

- name, address, contact numbers
- functions/skills analysis
- professional history
- educational history
- personal details.

Describing your skills

Look back at Part One (pages 28–29) where you outlined your key skills and competences. If you have used this information, you should already have sufficient information to work on. Select the skills and aptitudes you think are most relevant to this job.

When describing your skills, be precise. Many jobs will ask for candidates with good communication, organisation or presentation skills. To state that you are 'an effective communicator', 'are experienced in organising your workload' or are 'accustomed to giving presentations' is not enough. Anybody can make claims; what you need to give is evidence.

You may choose to summarise your strengths and achievements under headings for business functions or key skills. For example:

Marketing
Created programmes to develop new

market sectors; developed customer incentive schemes including the launch of a customer loyalty card; liaised with marketing and advertising agencies ...

Team skills
Developed and managed a team of seven marketing staff; responsibility for recruitment, selection and appraisal within my function; administered a staff training budget in excess of £85,000 and co-ordinated training across all functions.

Experience-based CV

Some job advertisements place a heavy emphasis on previous experience – or you may feel that your professional track record demands that you take an experience-based approach to your CV. In this case, your CV will follow this format:

- name, address and contact numbers
- opening statement of who you are
- career history
- educational history
- personal details.

Under each heading of your career history, include a summary of your main responsibilities and achievements. Set these out as bullet points.

1993–date Accountant XYZ Ltd

A retail organisation with 35 outlets across the UK, XYZ has a central accounts function in London. My role includes secondment to stores, branch auditing, payroll management and providing support to the selling function.

Responsibilities and achievements include:

- working with a team of three staff to investigate and reduce wastage by 30 per cent. This target was achieved within one year
- developing and delivering financial training to branch managers
- researching and recommending software for the accounts function
- administering annual audit procedures.

Check your CV

Before you send off your CV, use this checklist to make sure it is of a high enough standard.

CV CHECKLIST

✎ CV checked for:

☐ spelling

☐ grammar

☐ punctuation

☐ layout

☐ length (no more than two pages)

- [ ] information relevant to the job specification
- [ ] no unexplained gaps in work history
- [ ] claims for skills/competences are substantiated

APPLICATION FORMS

> **GOLDEN RULE 7**
>
> Successful job seekers understand how application forms work.

Application forms may be sent out by selectors who want specific information about candidates and a chance to see how you approach the vacancy. They are often used by large organisations, when a lot of applications are anticipated or a number of applications of very similar calibre are expected – for example, when recruiting graduates fresh from university.

From the selector's point of view, application forms have a number of advantages. They make it easier to compare data because it will be set out in the same format. The employer can present carefully focused questions. The application form provides a preselection test of written communication skills by supplying limited space in which the applicant must condense large amounts of information.

When you complete an application form it is unlikely you will know who is going to read it. Depending on the vacancy and the volume of replies, it may be considered by:

- a preselector within the company
- a line manager
- the selector
- an agency which has been asked to carry out this stage of the selection procedure.

In the first stages of selection, they will all be looking for similar information:

- Does this candidate meet the educational and professional requirements of the job?
- Does he/she comply with any age, nationality or location criteria?
- Does he/she have relevant experience?

The next stage will be to select applications which are particularly appropriate because they give evidence of the necessary qualifications, skills and experience. From these applications, selectors draw up a short list of candidates.

Before you start to complete any application form:

- check the deadline and don't miss it
- photocopy the form so that you can fill in a rough draft
- plan what you are going to say
- read the instructions – these may state, for example, that the form has to be handwritten, that you should use black ink, and certain sections must be completed in block capitals
- collect the data you need – this should already be stored in your personal databank

- allow yourself enough time – completing an application form well can take much longer than you anticipate.

The use of black ink is important since the application form may be photocopied for circulation within the organisation.

Application forms fall into two sections: the easy part and the difficult part.

The easy part

The first part of most application forms is straightforward. You will be asked to fill in your name, age, address, contact numbers, nationality, status, etc. You may also be asked where you heard about the vacancy. This is not a trick question to find out if you have inside information, it is simply a way for the organisation to analyse the effectiveness of its various recruitment methods.

Be systematic:

- follow the instructions, particularly for using block capitals
- don't leave gaps – write n/a if there is a section you cannot complete
- make sure that the dates of your education and work experience are accurate.

The difficult part

The questions in the second part of an application form ask you to expand on your skills and experience. Whatever the format of the questions – and they vary enormously – this will be the main intent. The statements that you make provide a basis for discussion at the interview.

Sample questions include:

- *Outline your main responsibilities in your present job.*
- *Describe a situation in which you have used your own initiative.*

What can you say that makes you stand out from the other applicants? Resist the temptation to make claims you cannot support. If you are called for interview you will be asked to elaborate on what you have written, a difficult task if you have not been absolutely truthful.

Look again at the job specification and your information about the organisation. What are they looking for? Tailor your comments accordingly to provide evidence that you meet their needs.

There may also be a section under the ambiguous heading of additional information:

If there is anything you wish to add in support of your application, please complete this section. Continue on another sheet if necessary.

Don't leave this blank. It is another opportunity to show your achievements, both work and non-work related. Keep your response relevant. If you use non-work achievements, ensure that they illustrate your skills base rather than just listing things you have done.

When you have completed the rough draft of the application form, check it for:

- spelling
- ambiguities
- missing information
- sufficiency – does it say enough about you?

Finally, ask yourself – 'Would I want to meet this person?' If you can, ask a partner or friend to read through the application form and give you an honest opinion.

Fill in the form, sign and date it. Before you send it off, take a photocopy. If you are called to interview, it will help if you know what you said at the preliminary selection stage. A photocopy will also help you fill in future application forms, but don't make the mistake of trying to use the same answers and format for every job application. Remember Rule 6; every job is different and your application form, like your CV, should reflect this.

Send in your application form with a covering letter which states:

- the job you are applying for
- who you are
- why your application is worth considering.

The covering letter should be brief, but it should also be strong enough to catch the preselector's eye. Again, make sure it is closely targeted to the job you are applying for. You will look at preparing letters next.

Finally, make a note of the closing date for applications. This gives you an idea of when you should hear something from the organisation. If you haven't had a reply within ten days of the closing date, you can start making follow-up calls.

COVERING LETTERS

> **GOLDEN RULE 8**
>
> Successful job seekers use covering letters to create impact.

Whether you are sending in an application form or a CV to a potential employer, it must be accompanied by a covering letter. As a first point of contact with a potential employer, this is one of the most important pieces of correspondence you will write. It should be succinct, stating clearly why you are writing, yet strong enough to make the recruiter select your application from the pile on the desk.

As with CVs, there is no standard letter that you can send out with all your correspondence. Every letter must be tailored to meet the needs of the employer and to fit the circumstances of your application.

With all correspondence, follow these conventions:

- use good quality white paper
- restrict the length of your letter to one page
- use plain, formal English and do not abbreviate words
- keep the content precise and closely targeted – don't waffle
- check that you have remembered to sign it using black ink
- use the correct salutation and closing – Dear Sir / Yours faithfully (see the next paragraph) Dear Mr Jones / Yours sincerely

- proofread before you put it in the envelope
- check layout – is the letter clear and visually pleasing?

Letters with application forms and CVs

Address the letter clearly to a named individual within the organisation. As we have already said, 'Dear Sir or Madam' is impersonal and your aim is to set up a degree of personal contact. There may be a named contact in the advertisement or job specification. If not, contact the organisation and find out the name of the human resources manager or the person in charge of recruitment.

State clearly which advertisement you are responding to. You may be asked to include a job code or reference number. You should also mention where you saw the advertisement since this helps recruiters monitor the success of their media advertising.

Be precise about the position for which you are applying. A large organisation may have a number of vacancies at the same time in the same function, or several jobs may be included within the same advertisement.

Now look back at the advertisement or job specification. What qualities and experience does the recruiter focus on? In your letter, highlight the ways in which your skills and experience match those the recruiter is seeking. Provide 'hooks' to catch the reader's attention and to interest them sufficiently to make them read through your application form.

Format

The format you use depends to some degree on your personal style. You may choose to list your relevant qualifications and experience as bullet points following an introductory sentence:

As my application form shows, I can offer:

- *five years' experience in providing administrative support to directors and managers*
- *a successful track record in training and motivating new staff*
- *fluency in Italian and French*
- *IT skills including database and spreadsheet management in Word and Lotus Smart Suite and WordPerfect.*

You could present the same information in short paragraphs – but limit yourself to no more than three.

As my application form indicates, for the past five years I have provided administrative support to the directors and senior managers at ABC Ltd. My responsibilities include managing a busy office with three staff, organising board meetings, reporting to shareholders and day-to-day management.

I have developed an induction scheme and implemented numerous training schemes for new staff. This includes both identifying off-the-job training opportunities and directing a mentoring programme.

I am fluent in French and Italian. My IT skills include word processing, spreadsheet and database management to NVQ Level 3,

> *as well as proficiency in Word, WordPerfect and Lotus Smart Suite.*

Your next paragraph should say briefly why you are applying for the position. You may well have expanded on this in the application form, so there is no need to go into detail. It is preferable to focus on positive reasons for wanting to move rather than expressing dissatisfaction with your current employer.

> *I am eager to move into a more responsible role with a larger company and believe I have the relevant skills and experience to contribute to the administrative function in your organisation.*

Make it clear in your final paragraph that you are looking forward to hearing from the recruiter and give details of how you can be contacted. This is particularly important if you cannot be contacted at work during the day.

Speculative letters

> *'I always read speculative letters and CVs and I have recruited on the strength of them. The letters that stand out are those which show some conviction – letters that indicate the writer knows something about our company and genuinely wants to work here. The other thing that gains a positive response is a follow-up telephone call. If applicants say they will phone, then I expect them to actually do it!'*

You will send out speculative letters because:

- you have been advised of a possible vacancy through a network contact

- you are targeting particular companies that work in your field
- you are targeting companies that you really want to work for
- you have identified, through your research, possible opportunities in companies you want to work for that are restructuring or expanding.

Keep the letter simple and straightforward. State clearly in the first paragraph why you are writing. This is particularly important in speculative letters where an approach which is too oblique could leave the reader in doubt as to who you are and what you want. Your reasons for writing could be:

I have always wanted to work for your company because ...

- *it is a market leader*
- *you are a respected and prominent employer in this field*
- *your company offers challenges and opportunities few employers can match.*

To get the reader's attention, you have to give them a reason for reading your letter. It works better to respond to their needs rather than outlining your own. What skills and expertise do you think this organisation might be looking for? Do these match your own, thus giving you a reason to draw yourself to their attention? If not, then you are probably targeting the wrong company.

With a speculative letter, avoid putting any pressure on the recipient. They have not advertised or publicised a vacancy so you are not responding to an expressed need. Make it absolutely clear that you are not expecting to be offered a job but that you are expressing an interest in the company.

You could suggest that:

- you are exploring opportunities within your profession
- you would like advice on the job market which they could supply
- you wish to be considered should an appropriate vacancy arise in the near future.

By making this clear, you are in a position to ask if you can make contact at a specified date to discuss job opportunities, or to ask that your details are kept on file for future reference. Be precise about what you want and what you intend to do.

> *I would welcome an opportunity to discuss the employment situation within ABC. I will telephone next Thursday morning between 10 a.m. and 11 a.m. to ask if we can arrange a meeting.*

This approach gives the recipient time to:

- decide on their response
- study your CV
- consider whether or not you are worth talking to
- identify opportunities for a meeting.

If the employer is not receptive to your application, then it saves embarrassment all round because they can simply write in reply before the date on which you plan to call – or arrange to be out of the office at the time you have specified!

Having said that you will telephone, make

sure you do. One senior outplacement consultant reports that 80 to 90 per cent of all speculative letter writers state that they will follow up with a call but very few of them actually do.

Do not place too much emphasis on network contacts unless you are absolutely sure they are sound. Writing that 'John Smith told me there might be a vacancy in your sales department' could land John Smith in a lot of trouble if his information is inaccurate. Similarly, playing on the friends' network can cause embarrassment if the employer has nothing to offer. If you have heard on the grapevine that a vacancy is coming up, by all means write in and send your CV, but leave the employer thinking it is the result of happy coincidence that your letter arrived at just the right time.

Follow-up letters

If you receive any feedback after sending off a speculative letter and CV, follow it up. If your initial letter results in a meeting, write a letter to your contact thanking them for their time and advice within two days of that meeting.

If you receive a letter saying 'thanks, but no thanks', it is still worth sending a brief note thanking them for reading through your details and asking to be kept on file. This is a simple, polite gesture that many people fail to make, so your conscientiousness will help you stand out from the rest. For the cost of half an hour's time and a first-class stamp, it could pay dividends in the long term by creating goodwill between you and the organisation.

Check your letter

Use this checklist to ensure that your letters are complete and well presented.

LETTER CHECKLIST

✎ Check your letter for:

- [ ] length (no more than one page)
- [ ] spelling
- [ ] punctuation
- [ ] grammar and plain English
- [ ] abbreviations (there shouldn't be any)
- [ ] short sentences
- [ ] correct salutation/close
- [ ] correct address
- [ ] date and signature
- [ ] vacancy stated
- [ ] reference number or code stated (if applicable)
- [ ] where you found the vacancy (if applicable)

Now reassess your letter in the light of these questions:

- Does it indicate how you match the desired criteria for the job?
- Does it state why you want to apply for the job?
- Does it point to your CV or application

form as a source of further information?
- Does it end on a positive note indicating what action you expect?
- Would *you* be interested in the person who wrote this letter?

So far in Part Two of *Job Seeking* you have considered ways of improving your written communication skills, particularly in relation to:

- your CV
- application forms
- covering letters.

There is, of course, another way of making preliminary contact. Some employers ask that candidates telephone for further information. Making such a call demands a whole new range of skills, which we shall look at next.

TELEPHONE SKILLS

GOLDEN RULE 9

Successful job seekers prepare before they pick up the phone.

The telephone can be one of your greatest allies during the job search. The problem is that many people still find telephone calls one of the most difficult forms of communication. When you pick up the phone and dial, you have no idea what the person on the other end of the line is doing. You can't see them so you cannot interpret their body language. You don't know whether they are genuinely pleased to hear from you or they are staring at the ceiling praying for you to finish the call. There are fewer indicators for you to work with, so you have to work harder.

Research suggests that during a telephone call, as little as 11 per cent of a message may actually be absorbed by the recipient so it is essential that your call is clear, focused and purposeful.

Think about reasons why you might use the phone as part of your job search. You could be:

- fixing up or confirming an appointment for interview
- asking for more information about the company as part of your pre-interview research
- 'cold-calling' to make contact with a potential employer
- taking part in a preliminary interview and being screened by the employer.

Whatever the reason, it is important to master the basic skills that contribute to your main objective, which is being in control of your telephone calls.

Making calls

1. Prepare before you pick up the telephone

Are you clear in your own mind what this call should achieve? Make a list of the information you want to obtain or the outcomes you are working towards. Preparation for a call also includes:

- having a pen and paper to hand so that you can make note of anything important
- having your CV or the relevant job advertisement in front of you so that you can answer any unexpected questions
- ensuring you have relevant data such as your e-mail address or your mobile phone number.

2. Choose your time

No, you can't predict the best time to call somebody – you don't know what they are doing, what mood they are in or what particular pressures they are facing when the telephone rings. It does make sense, however, to avoid some of the times when it will be most difficult to make contact.

Think about how you feel when you arrive at the office. After driving through the rush hour traffic or fighting the crowds on public transport, do you need half an hour and a cup of coffee to get yourself up to speed? Do you use the first hour of the day to prioritise your workload, check your correspondence and plan the rest of the day? Is that something you prefer to do without interruptions? The same principles may well apply to the person you are planning to telephone – so give them a chance to start the day before you call.

Similarly, a call just before lunch or last thing in the day may catch somebody just as they are ready to leave the office and not at their most receptive. Try calling mid-morning or early afternoon.

Always check that it is convenient to talk. If

it is not, then ask the person you are telephoning to specify a time when you can call back. Listen for indicators. Does the person sound harassed? Maybe you should call back later. Do they sound confused? Check you are speaking to the right person and that you have clearly explained why you are calling.

If you do get the impression that you have called at a bad time, don't take it personally. You can hardly be held responsible for their bad day since you haven't been anywhere near them. It's unfortunate to be at the receiving end of somebody else's bad mood but it happens. Stay calm and offer to call back at a more convenient time.

Finally make sure you call when *you* are not going to be interrupted. Avoid making the call just before you are expecting somebody to ring the doorbell or walk into your office.

3. Monitor your mood

Straight after a row with your partner, ten minutes after you receive a rejection letter or when you are simply feeling out of sorts with the world is not the best time to call a prospective employer. Your mood, your state of mind and your degree of enthusiasm can come over loud and clear through your voice. Pick a time to call when you are feeling positive and when you have the confidence to surmount any barriers.

4. Grin and bear it

In some ways, making telephone calls to prospective employers will become easier when we all have video phones. You will have to present yourself positively, smile and look your best every time you pick up the receiver. Until that day, it's worth remembering that your mood will affect your facial expression and that in turn will affect your tone of voice. When you give your greeting, smile. When you make a request, smile. When you're told that Mrs Brown can't take your call, smile. Smiling relaxes the muscles in your throat and face and consequently relaxes your vocal chords. Take a deep breath before you start and be enthusiastic. Your enthusiasm will communicate itself over the telephone.

5. Be confident

You have a valid reason for calling. Don't apologise. 'I'm sorry to bother you but ... ' is one of the most irritating telephone phrases. If you're sorry, why are you doing it? Your confidence should be reflected in the way you speak – purposeful sentences, clearly structured requests. Try not to let your sentences trail away or to 'hum and hah'.

6. Pace yourself

The speed at which you speak and the pace of your delivery is doubly important when you have only your voice with which to communicate. Face-to-face you can read the other person's expression to see when you are going too fast. A slight frown, a raised eyebrow or hand and you know you need to slow down. There are no such visual cues on the phone. In addition, nervousness can lead you to speak more quickly and your conversation may degenerate into an irritating round of repetition and misunderstanding.

Make your introductory remarks fairly

slowly so that the other person can tune into the conversation and work out who you are and why you are calling. Speak clearly and audibly. Don't ask more than one question at a time and take note of the answer before you move to the next subject.

7. Introduce yourself

Start any call by stating clearly your name. Then, if you are not sure, ask the name of the person with whom you are speaking and check what role they play in the organisation.

8. Listen

In your anxiety to make an impression or to get information, don't forget to listen carefully to what is being said. Can you get any pointers from tone of voice or speed of speech as to what the other person is thinking? Use the telephone for dialogue, not monologue.

Make the listening process easier by cutting out any background noise that might distract you. Turn off the radio or CD and put the dog and the children in another (preferably soundproofed) room.

9. Confirm

You have your pen and paper to hand, so use them. Note any names, dates, times and other relevant information as you talk. Before you close the conversation, repeat key information to make sure you have it exactly right. Check the spellings of names and addresses if you plan to write a letter to this person or organisation at a later date.

Prepare for your call

Use this checklist to prepare for a telephone call. Write next to the first five headings *before* you make contact.

TELEPHONE CALL CHECKLIST

Name of organisation:

Name of contact:

Objective of the call:

Information I need from them:

Information I want to give to them:

Action required after the call:

Anticipate their response

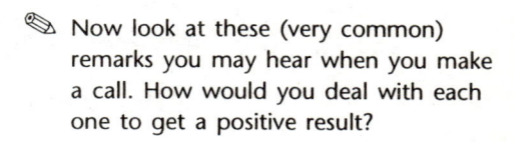

- Now look at these (very common) remarks you may hear when you make a call. How would you deal with each one to get a positive result?

- 'I'm sorry, she's in a meeting.'
- 'Mr Cranfield is away until next week.'
- 'What can I do for you?'
- 'I think you are through to the wrong department.'

SUMMARY

Part Two of *Job Seeking* has taken you through various steps for making initial contact with employers. In particular, it addressed your written communication and telephone skills. These are both areas in which practice pays off. Build up these skills and you can be confident that your application merits a response.

Part Three takes you one step nearer to your goal of getting the job you want by examining the selection procedure in some detail. It provides valuable advice on both preparing for interview and improving your interview skills.

Part three

STEP BY STEP

Almost all employers will use an interview as part of their selection process. Nobody can predict how that interview will go on the day. Talk to anybody who has been through more than one interview and you'll hear the disaster stories:

- 'The car broke down and I arrived an hour late'.
- 'I expected to be interviewed by the managing director and found myself in front of a panel of four.'
- 'They asked me questions I just couldn't answer.'
- 'I accepted a cup of coffee, choked on the first sip and spent the next two minutes coughing.'

Even if you don't get the job, you should at least come out of the room knowing you gave a creditable performance. It is possible to improve the odds of an interview being a successful, positive encounter. As with every step in the job search, a successful interview involves thorough preparation.

Part Three of *Job Seeking* takes you through a number of steps involved in that preparation. These include:

- analysing the interview process
- looking at different styles of interview, including assessment centres and tests
- researching the organisation
- thinking about interview questions.

Next you will focus on interview skills and consider ways to:

- create a positive first impression

- improve your verbal communication skills
- use and interpret body language and non-verbal communication skills.

THE INTERVIEW PROCESS

GOLDEN RULE 10

Successful job seekers prepare thoroughly before the interview.

In Part Two you looked at the recruitment and selection processes from the employer's perspective. By understanding how these systems work, you can use them to your own advantage. Consequently, appreciating how employers interview will help prepare you for situations that arise when you enter the interview room. What are prospective employers looking for when they interview? How does the interview work for them?

All interviews are different and it is impossible to describe here all the possible styles and procedures you might encounter. What this book can do is outline some of the most typical formats and likely situations in which you could find yourself.

To get to the point where you are invited for interview, you have successfully completed some sort of preselection process. This involved an examination of your CV or application form, a telephone interview or an assessment centre (see page 108). That does not mean the people who are responsible for filling the job vacancy know anything about you. Preselection may have been carried out by a junior member of the organisation, by an independent agency, or even by a computer.

The day before the interview may be the first time the interviewers really get a chance to think about the candidates. If they are lucky, they will have a synopsis of the various candidates which highlights particular areas where they meet the needs of the job. If they are less fortunate, they will have only a copy of a CV or application form and will be interviewing with little detailed knowledge of the candidates.

Who interviews?

Interviews can involve almost anybody. You may find yourself in front of line managers, senior management, directors, peers, support staff or human resource specialists. There have also been reports of the managing director's spouse, an astrologer and a dog being present at interviews. (The rationale with the latter was (a) the company owner always brought the dog to work, and (b) if a candidate could deal with the dog's presence, then he or she could probably cope with the demands of the job.)

Many organisations now train their staff in interview techniques. If you are applying to such an organisation, the process should be much easier for everybody involved – including you.

> 'We train our staff to interview because we believe that for an interview to be effective, the candidates have to be able to present themselves positively. They can't do that if

> they feel intimidated. Our interviewers know
> how to establish a rapport and put the
> applicants at ease by using their verbal skills
> and body language positively. But being
> relaxed doesn't mean they are not observing
> the candidate very closely.'

If, however, your prospective employer is inexperienced in interviewing, then you could face one of the following problems:

- lack of planning so the interviewers don't really know what they are looking for
- interruptions from other people throw you off balance
- an interview that does not run to plan and becomes too much of an informal chat
- interviewers who are too subjective and rely purely on gut reaction
- a superficial interview that does not probe your suitability for the job
- an interview that is too complex, focusing on some areas but not giving a wider picture of your skills and experience.

Specific problems you might come up against include:

Mirroring – interviewers may subconsciously favour a candidate who mirrors themselves in background, appearance and behaviour. Think of all the organisations you have come across that appear to be staffed by clones and you will see the effects of mirroring. Mirroring can have a negative effect on your job chances if you remind the interviewer of somebody they *don't* like. Help the situation by keeping your body language positive, listening carefully to what the interviewer says and responding clearly to their questions. If you sense a degree of antipathy, don't respond aggressively.

Logical error – where the interviewer assumes something you do or say has a specific reason. For example, you may have advanced rapidly within an organisation because it has a high staff turnover and a policy of recruiting from within. To the interviewer this may be a sign of commendable ambition. (Logical error, used carefully, can occasionally be used to your advantage!) If you suspect the interviewer misunderstands what you are saying, check by rephrasing and repeating, but try not to state openly that they have made a mistake.

Superficiality – the interviewer does not know which questions to ask to probe beneath the surface, or alternatively may be uncomfortable with the whole interview process and too anxious to help you perform well. In this case it is up to you to monitor the interview and check you have given them all the information they need to make their decision.

You will read more about using communication and non-verbal communication skills later in Part Three.

WHICH STYLE OF INTERVIEW

When you arrive for interview, you could find yourself:

- in a **one-to-one interview**, where you talk to one selector
- in a **panel interview**. A number of

selectors form a panel. Each may represent a different function within the organisation and look at a different aspect of your performance. Because of the difficulties of getting a number of interviewers together at the same time, you will probably be interviewed on the same day as other applicants
- **seeing several people sequentially**. This system lets several different people assess the candidate and allows for a combined decision. Again, a number of other applicants will be interviewed on the same day. Each interviewer will look at a different area of experience. A sequential interview programme may look like this:

Time	Interviewer	Subject
2.00	Managing director	Career history
2.30	Line manager	Technical and professional abilities
3.00	HR manager	Development potential

THE STAGES OF THE INTERVIEW

An interview should follow three distinct stages.

1. Meet and greet

This stage is designed to put you at your ease and establish a rapport between both parties. You will be introduced to the interviewer(s), who will explain the objectives of the interview and roughly how long it will take. Any questions at this stage will be straightforward and direct. You may also be given some background about the job and the organisation.

2. In-depth questioning

At the second stage, the questions take on more depth. Questions can combine different styles:

- **open questions** that ask for a detailed response. You could be asked to provide evidence of your achievements and skills, to expand on points made in your CV or to give opinions
- **closed questions** are designed to extract information and confirm understanding. Usually they involve a fairly short yes/no answer
- **leading questions** which again ask for your opinions but are phrased in such a way that you may think you know what the interviewer wants to hear. Beware of these; interviewers should be trained not to ask them.

There is more on questions and questioning techniques later in Part Three.

3. Summary and close

The third stage of the interview brings the procedure to a close. At this point you have a chance to ask questions and to emphasise points you think are important. It is also an opportunity for the interviewer to convince you that you want the job so you may discuss salary, procedures and contracts.

This is your final opportunity to impress, to highlight your strengths and to recap on your suitability for the post.

ASSESSMENT CENTRES

Many large organisations will not only interview, they will also invite you to take part in an assessment centre. An assessment centre is not a place, it is a process. A number of applicants for a position (or for a number of jobs within the same organisation) will be asked to gather together to undergo a series of tests. They will be evaluated by trained assessors against a predetermined list of job-related criteria.

This type of selection originated in the armed forces and civil service where large numbers of recruits were needed. It has become increasingly common in large organisations. In many ways, it is the most accurate and objective way of predicting performance and analysing a candidate's suitability. So why don't more employers use assessment centres? Quite simply, they can be very expensive to organise and run.

Specialist companies are often employed to administer assessment centres. Their staff should have the necessary skills to carry out a fair and objective assessment. On the other hand, they will not be able to tell you about the job so don't go in expecting to get more information on the position or the company to which you are applying.

From the employer's standpoint the assessment centre can provide valuable information that might not come through in an interview. It shows candidates in action and illustrates how they work in groups. It is a useful method of testing problem-solving abilities and interpersonal skills and, perhaps most importantly, it shows how candidates react to challenges without being given long periods for preparation.

Despite the testing nature of an assessment centre, it can be an enjoyable experience, particularly if you can get over the competitive nature of the selection process and work *with* the other candidates. The tests which assessors run will vary and some of them can be both interesting and fun.

An assessment centre is only one part of the selection process and is unlikely to be used as the sole means of selection. However, if you are invited to an assessment centre, you need to perform well in order to make it to the interview.

What to expect

So, what can you expect when you turn up for an assessment centre? A number of different activities are carried out, usually through a full day or half day. If it is a full day session, you'll probably get lunch – and may find yourself scrutinised by the assessors as you eat. Their brief is to find out more about the 'real you' in all situations, including those that are not official exercises.

Activities fall into two categories:

- tests
- simulations and exercises.

Tests can comprise numerical, verbal reasoning, ability, aptitude and personality assessments. Exercises include some for you as an individual and some for the whole group. However odd the tasks may appear, don't be fooled. They all have a purpose and the assessment centre will have been carefully structured to provide a detailed analysis of how you match the requirements of the job. For example, if an employer has drawn up a person specification for a job that demands good communication, team working and leadership skills, each criterion will be tested a number of times in a variety of situations. This not only checks your performance but also gives you more than one chance to show that you meet those criteria.

This matrix illustrates how activities may be planned:

	In tray exercise	Group problem	Role play (meeting)
Decision making	*	*	*
Team working		*	*
Communication skills	*	*	*

Exercises are usually based on the type of activities you will face in the job. Don't let that put you off if you are applying for a position that involves a change in career direction. Your technical expertise is less important than your skills at this stage.

Here are examples of specific exercises and ways you can approach them.

In tray exercise

This is usually an individual exercise designed to consider your organisational skills, your ability to prioritise and to delegate. You may be presented with an in tray comprising correspondence, memos and other information with which you are expected to work. As the new employee, it is your job to sort through the bundle deciding how you will handle each task, who you might refer to and which tasks take precedence. You may be asked to talk through your actions at the end of a given period of time, or the assessors will take the in tray away and look through it later. In either case, make clear notes of questions and action on each piece of correspondence.

Tips for in tray exercises

- Read through all the correspondence first.
- Prioritise – put all papers in order of importance.
- Work through each one systematically.
- Aim to identify a clear course of action.
- Don't spend too much time on any one piece of correspondence – keep an eye on the clock.
- Make clear notes on each paper under headings such as task, contacts, action.

Group discussion

Candidates are brought together in small groups to work as a committee or project team. They will be given one or more items to discuss, asked to resolve a problem and decide on a course of action. Within your group, you may be given a specific role or you may all have the same information and function. Assessors will be looking at your communication skills (that includes your ability to listen as well as talk), group interaction and negotiation skills as well as your problem-solving skills.

Tips for group discussions
- Listen carefully to instructions.
- Make sure you understand what you have to do.
- Be prepared to listen to other members of the group.
- Respect their opinions even if you don't agree with them.
- Avoid dominating the session but do make some contribution.
- Keep the end result in sight and watch the clock – your group must provide some resolution to the problem.

Simulations and role play

These take a number of different forms. For example, you may be given a problem to work on and told that you will be allowed to interview a member of staff who is involved with the situation. Your brief is to gather information to make a decision. After 15–20 minutes' preparation time, you discuss the problem with the member of staff (a role player). This may be followed by a full group meeting when all of you report back on the action you decided to take. Assessors consider the ways in which you prepared for the interview, your communication and problem-solving skills. Don't be surprised if, when you report back to the full group, you find that you have all been given a slightly different perspective on the problem.

Tips for role play

- Enter into the spirit of the exercise.
- Use the preparation time to list questions and objectives.
- Listen carefully to the information you are given.
- Don't jump to conclusions.
- Be prepared to present your findings to an assessor (or to the group as a whole) and to explain how you came to a conclusion.

Analysis exercise

Working alone, you will be given a case study on which to work and asked to make a decision. You will be given factual information, some of which may be difficult to analyse or appear contradictory. For example, you could receive a body of information about a member of staff who has not been performing satisfactorily. This includes both positive and negative reports and opinions. You must decide on a course of action. At the end of a given period of time, you will communicate your decision through a brief presentation to the assessors or by preparing a written report.

Assessors will look at your ability to process and analyse information, the methods you use to work through the problem and resolve it, and your presentation skills.

Tips for analysis exercises

- Read through all the information first.
- Make sure you are clear about what you must do.
- Plan your time so that you can prepare adequately for your presentation or write your report.
- Don't jump to conclusions.
- Avoid making subjective decisions.
- Justify every step you take.

'I took part in an assessment centre with ten other candidates. Initially it was disconcerting having this group of assessors sitting around the room furiously scribbling notes on our performance but after a while I forgot about them. Some of the activities were sound and others were really irritating – 'bloody Blue Peter' as one of the other candidates put it. There was a temptation to play to the gallery and give the assessors what they wanted. I remember sitting through a group discussion and being very diplomatic when under normal circumstances I would have shouted the others down. But I guess the assessors are trained to spot a phoney and there was such a variety of things to do that they had a fair chance of weighing us all up.'

Assessment

To perform well at an assessment centre you need to understand what the assessors are looking for. They are not playing 'spot the weakness' but giving you a chance to demonstrate your strengths. Your performance will be assessed over the whole session. Because the structure of the exercises are designed to test each skills area more than once, performing badly in one exercise will not automatically rule out your candidacy for the job.

TESTS

As part of an assessment centre, or during an interview with an organisation, you may have to complete one or more tests. Used correctly, tests give an objective assessment of applicants' abilities in a number of different fields. Properly administered, tests produce impartial results based on ability, not on sex, age, race or background.

Tests are devised and published by specialist companies which employ occupational psychologists to construct and evaluate them. Accredited tests will have been extensively tested and verified through pilot schemes. Ideally, experts will be on hand to administer tests and to ensure the correct test systems are chosen for a particular selection procedure. However, some companies, having bought in the tests, prefer to administer them in-house. They should do this using trained and accredited assessors.

Employers use tests for a number of reasons. Practical, job-related tests may be used to check your skills and proficiency within a certain field of work. For example, somebody applying to an agency for clerical or secretarial work may have to complete a word processing test to assess their speed and accuracy.

Secondly, tests help an employer collect more information about the applicant's core skills such as numeracy, literacy and problem solving. A GCE in Maths in 1985 does not necessarily reflect your mathemtical skills in 1999, and if the job involves analysing or using figures then the employer may want to test now to get a more accurate view of your proficiency.

Thirdly, some employers use specially designed tests which theoretically profile aspects of your personality, such as your ability to work in teams or work on your own initiative. Should an employer use tests as part of the selection procedure then you may be asked to complete a range of different styles of tests, spending a fixed amount of time on each type.

Types of tests

There are three main types of tests: ability, aptitude and personality tests.

Ability tests

These assess your visual awareness, numerical and verbal reasoning powers. You may be asked to complete:

- **abstract tests**, which typically ask you to find differences or similarities between groups of patterns, number sequences, etc.
- **verbal reasoning exercises**, which test your skill in making sense of reports and written information by relating it to a set of questions. The passages you read may not be straightforward and could contain contradictions or inaccuracies. Your task demands that you use the information to evaluate whether statements are

true or false or whether you have insufficient information to make a judgement
- **numerical tests**, which evaluate your ability to reason using numerical information presented in different forms such as text, graphs or tables.

Aptitude tests

Aptitude tests assess your problem-solving skills or test your ability to carry out a particular function. As well as contributing to the profile of your skills, both ability and aptitude tests are considered to be indicators of future performance.

Personality tests

These work on the principle that our performance at work depends on more than just abilities and aptitudes. Personality tests are used to gain some idea of your motivation, self-confidence, style of working, team abilities, etc. All of these factors can influence your performance in the workplace.

Typically you may be asked to indicate with which of two statements you most identify, to grade statements on a scale according to whether you support them or not, and to select words which reflect aspects of your personality.

Doing the tests

The format and way in which tests are delivered depends on the individual organisation. However, taking a positive approach to the tests can help your performance.

Attitude

The employer who asks you to complete a series of tests has chosen this as a selection method. That is their prerogative. Whether you agree or disagree with testing is irrelevant – this is not a time for your cynicism to show. The tests are important, so treat them seriously.

Remember that tests have been developed by experts and go beyond the 'pop psychology' quizzes of mass market magazines. A well-devised test does not let you predict the answers.

Read the instructions

Before you begin, check that you fully understand what you have to do. If you are asked to score statements on a ranking scale of 1–5, is 1 high or low? How are you expected to record your responses?

You will usually be given time before the test begins to familiarise yourself with the type of questions. You may be given a sample paper which you can examine. If you have any doubts about the contents, ask for clarification.

Timing

Tests, particularly those designed to prepare personality profiles, often demand that you answer a large number of questions in a short period of time. The aim is to get an honest 'knee-jerk' response rather than to give you time to weigh up the pros and cons of an argument. Follow the instructions and mark down the response that best fits your opinion, then move on to the next question. You are not expected to evaluate or think in any depth.

Similarly in numeracy and literacy tests, you may be working against the clock. Do not spend too much time on any one question. If you finish early you can return and check your answers or fill in any missed responses. Put down answers even if you are not sure whether they are correct. You could be right – and a wrong response will not penalise you any more than a missed response does.

After the test

You should be given some feedback on your test results and an opportunity to discuss the insights these tests provide. British Mensa, which has moved into the area of psychometric testing, strongly advocates that information is shared between those taking and administering the tests.

> *'At first, the idea of sitting tests was awful – it took me right back to my schooldays. But these tests were different. I knew they were only part of the selection procedure so I had other chances to show my abilities. The psychological tests were particularly interesting because the selectors actually talked through the results with us. I was surprised how accurately their conclusions reflected aspects of my personality.'*

So far in Part Three you have looked at some of the ways in which interviews work. How can you use this knowledge to your advantage? The answer is straightforward. Prepare, prepare, then prepare some more.

DO YOUR RESEARCH

Now that you are familiar with typical interview formats, you can take a number of steps to ensure that you are ready for your first meeting with the selectors.

Research the company

GOLDEN RULE 11

Successful job seekers are well informed about the organisations to which they apply.

In this age of information, it is not difficult to find out something about a prospective employer. Taking time to find out all you can gives you an additional advantage in that you can talk intelligently about the organisation. It also shows that you have a degree of commitment to the job search and have taken time to do your homework – an attitude that should impress the interviewer.

Aim to find out about the organisation's:

- major functions or products
- financial performance
- growth
- locations and number of staff
- position in the marketplace
- major competitors.

Sources of information about the organisation include:

- company reports and financial statements
- public relations brochures

- publications such as company histories
- market or sector analyses by research organisations (such as Mintel)
- trade directories and registers.

These are easy enough to access. You can try:

- ringing the company and asking for any publications they can send you – few organisations will refuse
- talking to your contacts who work for or have worked for the organisation; bear in mind that the information they give you may be subjective, so try to distinguish between useful facts and their opinions
- looking in the reference section at the library
- using the Internet.

The Internet is one of your most valuable research tools because it presents you with large volumes of information quickly. Web sites from individual organisations should include the latest data on the company's performance, products and specialisms. They may also have staff profiles. Some companies will present information on jobs that are currently available together with detailed job specifications. Don't just look at the sort of jobs *you* want. By checking out other areas of employment you will find out a lot about the company's management style, its mission and the directions it intends to take.

Research the job

If you have been called to interview then you must already display qualities the company is seeking. Re-read the job description. Are there any areas about which you are unclear? Use the profile on pages 28–29 to compare your competences with the ones the company has requested. If there are shortfalls, have you overlooked areas of your own experience that might be relevant and that you could mention at the interview?

Prepare for the selectors' questions

> **GOLDEN RULE 12**
>
> Successful job seekers think about their responses before the interview.

Preparing a script to get you through the interview is unlikely to help your performance and may throw you off balance when you are asked a question you did not anticipate. Re-reading your CV and thinking about your employment and personal history will help to prepare your thoughts before the interview, however. Interviewers will ask you to expand on some of the points you outlined in your CV or application form, such as:

- your skills:
  - management and organisational skills
  - communication skills
  - leadership skills
  - interpersonal skills

- your career history:
  - key achievements
  - job-related competences
  - current (or most recent) job

- previous jobs
- particular projects
- career plan

- your personal and professional development:
  - educational background
  - job-related training
  - personal development

- you:
  - personal circumstances
  - outside interests
  - ambitions
  - strengths
  - weaknesses.

✎ Take each of these topics and make brief notes to clarify your responses. Refer to the competence profile you prepared on pages 28–29 to refresh your memory on your strengths. When you answer questions during your interview, the emphasis should be on giving evidence to show what you have done. For example, under personal and professional development:

- **Educational background** – as personal databank. Note special areas of interest followed through diploma and Master's courses.
- **Job-related training** – list of courses (personal databank).
- **Personal development** – Open University MBA started in 1996. Reasons – personal satisfaction and a desire to get a more complete picture of how business works. Have developed a regular study programme

in my own time – good discipline.
- **Intentions** – to extend my knowledge of team building and project management skills – both would be relevant to my work.

Twenty questions you could be asked at interview

This list has been compiled from the experience of candidates for a wide range of jobs. It is by no means definitive and it may be that at your interview none of these come up. Nevertheless, these are the type of questions interviewers ask and they will help you focus your thoughts as you prepare for interview.

1. Why do you want this job?
2. Why are you looking for another job?
3. What elements of your current job do you find most satisfying?
4. What frustrates you in your present job?
5. What particular strengths can you bring to this company?
6. What attracts you to this company?
7. Describe a situation which illustrates your project management/communication, etc. skills.
8. Describe a particular problem you faced and how you resolved it.
9. Where do you see yourself in five years' time?
10. How would your colleagues describe you?

11. What do you think are your greatest strengths?

12. What do you consider to be your weaknesses?

13. What do you know about this company?

14. How would you tackle this situation: [*Given a sample scenario*]

15. How would you develop your department?

16. How do you respond to change?

17. How do you see your career developing?

18. Tell me about yourself. [*Not a good question, but it does come up*]

19. Describe your career to date. [*Also a tricky one*]

20. What do you do when you are not working? [*Use your discretion when you answer this one!*]

How to answer questions

In the next section on interview skills, you'll find out more about dealing with questions when you are actually sitting in the interview room. If you are thinking about answers at this stage, remember to:

- give evidence – claims are nothing if they cannot be substantiated. What you have done counts for more than what you think you can do
- be honest – you will gain nothing in the long run by pretending to be somebody you are not
- be succinct – answer the questions. Don't

use the interview as a platform for a speech, and stick to the point
- be positive – even when discussing your weaknesses, you are showing awareness of yourself which means you can improve – and that is a valuable attribute
- be confident – modesty may be an appealing trait in the very famous and the very rich and one that you normally choose to adopt in your everyday life. The interview, however, is the last chance you have to sell yourself to a potential employer and by being too modest you may well undersell yourself. Have confidence in your own abilities and don't be afraid to state them
- avoid arrogance.

'I interviewed a candidate last year for a position in the HR division of the company. She was well qualified and although she had only been in employment for four years, she was obviously going places. Unfortunately she was trying to get there too quickly. Everything, from her body language to her tone of voice to her use of every acronym and jargon phrase possible, showed that she thought the job was hers. No doubt she intended to take my job over, too.'

Prepare an example

You could be asked to explain how you handled a particular problem or challenge in your present or most recent job. Think about that question now. A brief, off the cuff answer is not enough.

✎ Use these headings to draft out a more detailed response for your own reference. This will help you to explain not only *what* you did but *why* and *how* you did it.

- What was the problem or challenge?
- Who was involved?
- What was the objective?
- What obstacles did you face?
- How did you approach the issue?
- What data did you use?
- What business principles did you apply?
- How did you manage any change that was involved?
- How did you manage the other people involved?
- How was the situation resolved?
- How do you view this resolution?
- How would you act differently if faced with a similar situation again?

Prepare your own questions

The interview is a two-way process. Not only does it give the employer an opportunity to consider you for the vacancy, it also gives you a chance to assess the company as a potential employer. In their enthusiasm to 'get the job', this is an aspect many job seekers overlook. However, if you accept a job that is not right for you, within months you could be job seeking again. That will have severe cost implications for the employer – and put you back where you started with a questionable section on your CV marked 'most recent employment – six months'.

Preparing for an interview involves researching the company. Use the interview as an opportunity to find out more, particularly about the function within which you will work, the job itself and your fellow employees. Don't be afraid to ask some hard questions. It is in your own interests to find out as much as you can – and that may include bad news as well as good.

Twenty questions you might want to ask at interview

1. Why has this vacancy arisen?
2. What happened to the previous job holder?
3. What is the company's management structure?
4. What is the company's management style?
5. What will the job involve?
6. How are targets set?
7. What can I expect to be working on during my first month?
8. Who will I work with?
9. Who do I report to?
10. Where will I work?
11. What facilities and support are available?
12. What opportunities will there be for training and development?
13. What opportunities are there for advancement?

14. What are the company's long and short-term objectives?

15. How is performance measured?

16. Are there any structural or organisational changes in the pipeline?

17. What are the key issues the company is now facing?

18. How is salary determined?

19. When would I be expected to start work?

20. How soon will you make your selection?

Clarify the details

Preparing for interview means taking care of details, however minor these may seem.

Ask for clear instructions on where the interview will take place. If you are not familiar with the location, do a dummy run a few days beforehand. Not only will this eradicate any last minute panic when you take a wrong turning, it will also help you to estimate exactly how much time you need to allow for your journey.

If your interview takes place in the morning some distance from home, then consider making the journey the day before and staying overnight. The interview will be stressful enough without adding the strain of a rush hour journey into unknown territory.

You should have a written record of the time of interview. If arrangements were made over the telephone, ring the day before to confirm.

'An editor with a large publishing company asked me to go down to see her. We made the arrangement before Christmas for a date in January and foolishly I didn't check that the interview was still on before I set off from home. I went down the day before and booked into a hotel – both at my own expense. The following morning I was already on my way to the company headquarters when my mobile phone rang. It was somebody from the publishing company ringing to cancel the meeting, as the woman I was due to see had relocated to New York and nobody else knew why she had arranged to see me. As I was already at the gates, somebody agreed to see me. I spent an uncomfortable half hour trying to explain my work to a rather disinterested person who had only started work the previous week. Needless to say, I never heard from them again and I went home £130 out of pocket. I was annoyed that they didn't contact me earlier to let me know the meeting was off. I was equally annoyed with myself for not ringing a couple of days earlier to confirm.'

This may seem like a lot of preparation for one short interview but it will pay off. Being adequately prepared puts you in control and will stop you panicking if the unexpected happens.

Many of these steps will become automatic after a period of time – you will not have to remind yourself to check the location of the interview or think about interview questions the night before. But do remember that every interview will be different so you need to spend time planning your responses.

Next, Part Three focuses on the interview itself, particularly the skills you need to get you through the time you spend with the selectors.

INTERVIEW SKILLS

Assuming you are thoroughly prepared, the groundwork has been done. Now you must give a good performance and communicate to the interviewers just how capable you are. Improving your interview skills will help.

A confident approach

> **GOLDEN RULE 13**
>
> Successful job seekers know that first impressions count.

There is a saying in the retail industry: 'It takes one minute to make an impression and a lifetime to get over it.' Impressions made in the first minutes of an interview can dictate your success or failure in getting a job. It follows, therefore, that the way you look is one of the most powerful weapons in your job-seeking artillery. Your aim is to look professional and in control so you must appear well-groomed. Simple common sense rules apply:

- plan your wardrobe well before the date of the interview and lay your clothes out the night before

- check that you have spares of anything that could get marked or damaged on the way to the interview such as tights or stockings or a tie
- bear in mind the uncertainties of the English weather and plan for all eventualities – are you equipped to deal with a sudden rain shower or change in temperature?

There are countless articles and books on dressing for success. The recommendations they make are usually very sound and if you are uncertain about your own style, taking advice from either a book or a style consultant will be a good investment. You are probably familiar with the basics:

- wear smart, discreet clothing
- avoid any outfit that feels tight or constrictive
- choose muted colours that suit your colouring
- try to avoid brand new clothes – being comfortable will boost your confidence
- keep jewellery to a minimum
- people really do look at your feet – make sure shoes are clean and in a good state of repair.

The way you dress should suit you. If you try to disguise yourself through your outfit, it simply won't work. Bear in mind the nature of the organisation as well: are they more likely to go for 'corporate smart' or respect an expression of individuality? If you are applying for a post with a young and trendy design company famous for its informal approach, will they be looking for a 'suit'?

'We were interviewing for a junior manager.

The third candidate was well-dressed – dark suit, white shirt and discreetly patterned tie – and he was carrying a crumpled plastic carrier bag. He put it down beside his chair and I couldn't take my eyes off it. It seemed totally at odds with both the interview and the candidate himself. Had he suddenly opened the bag and produced a portfolio, he might have redeemed the situation, but he didn't. I was dying to ask him what was in there but that seemed intrusive. Plus, had he said it was his shopping or his overnight things, we would have both been embarrassed. So I said nothing and at the end of the interview he picked up the carrier bag and left. No, he didn't get the job – one of the other candidates was better qualified and had more relevant experience. But that carrier bag stuck in my mind for months. It seemed so very unprofessional.'

When you arrive for the interview

Arrive too early and you will be walking the streets. Arrive late and you start the interview at a disadvantage. Aim to reach the location of the interview about 10–15 minutes before the given time.

If you are shown into a waiting area, check for any company literature or magazines and flick through them. It will help you to 'think yourself' into the company. If you need to, take a final look at your CV and briefing notes. Don't be afraid to take these with you into the interview if you feel that they will help your presentation. An experienced interviewer will accept that you may need to refer to your own notes, particularly when you get to ask the questions.

In the first few minutes after you enter the building, forget the interview and see the place from the perspective of a client. Do you like the look and feel of this place?

- What is the atmosphere of the company when you walk in (busy, quiet, empty, overcrowded)?
- How are you greeted by the reception staff (welcoming, dismissive, busy, bored, curious)?
- What are the surroundings like (smart, scruffy)?

Ask yourself: Can I work here? Your first impressions count, so don't disregard your instinctive reaction to the workplace.

Be aware of the other people around you such as the reception staff and make an effort to acknowledge and greet them. They could be your colleagues in the near future.

When you enter the interview room

You want to create a strong – but not overbearing – first impression through your words and the way you move. As you enter the room:

- take a deep breath
- put your shoulders back and lift your chin
- smile
- make eye contact with all the people inside the room
- acknowledge each person individually with a smile
- as introductions are made, give a firm (but not bone-crushing) handshake

- listen as the introductions are made. You need to remember the name and function of every person there
- let the interviewer indicate where you should sit.

If you are facing a panel of interviewers, spread your attention between all the members. Don't become too focused on any one individual, however dominant they might be.

During the interview

There may be a few confident, blessed individuals who genuinely enjoy interviews. There are probably many more who say they enjoy the challenge but really find interviews as stressful as the rest of us. For most people, an interview is on par with an examination in terms of the insecurity, stress and panic it can cause.

Stress before and during an interview is a normal reaction. Stress can make you more alert and stimulate you to perform well. It focuses your attention and keeps you alert. At the same time, it can:

- make you appear argumentative and aggressive
- render you almost silent
- lead you to say too much
- make you feel vulnerable.

Stress can be controlled. Your aim is to calm yourself before you go into the interview room, to appear assertive and confident when you are in there and to retain a degree of control whatever the interviewers throw at you.

> *'At the beginning of the interview, we tell candidates exactly what is going to happen. We explain the types of questions we will be asking, the sort of information we are looking for and how long the interview will last. I can usually tell which candidates have spent some time thinking about their responses before the interview because they visibly start to relax.'*

Be assertive

Remember:

- aggressive behaviour promotes conflict
- passive behaviour promotes negativity
- assertive behaviour promotes co-operation.

Assertiveness involves respecting the rights of others and knowing that they respect your rights. Assertive behaviour in an interview:

- makes you appear confident
- helps you feel better about yourself
- leads others to respect you
- encourages others to listen to you
- helps you to achieve what you want – in this case, the offer of a job.

You communicate assertiveness through both non-verbal communication and speech. We look at both of these in more detail later.

Remember your preparation

In the section on preparing for interview, you looked at some of the formats interviews might take and considered how to deal with situations that could arise. Now that you are actually in the room, your preparation should pay off by increasing your confidence and improving your performance. Don't forget that the interview is a two-way process designed not only to assess your suitability for the job but to give *you* a chance to consider whether this company is the employer you want.

What do you want to know?

You have already looked at a number of questions you might want to ask during your interview. Use this time with the employer to clarify:

- responsibilities
- salary and benefits package
- targets
- management structure
- training opportunities
- opportunities for advancement.

You want to get a feel for life in this company and a realistic picture of what your role will be.

Be alert for any hidden agenda. Are you missing something? Will the job make demands on your time and capabilities that you will not be able to meet?

Listen to the answers. However much you want the job, it has to be right for you. Taking the wrong job will get you nowhere.

Humour

Have you heard about the candidate who told the joke about his last employer and the Pekinese and didn't get the job? An experienced interviewer will put you at your ease and help you to relax. In a relaxed atmosphere, some levity is a normal reaction, even if it is little more than a smile and an ironic comment on the traffic on the M25. Forced or scripted humour, deliberate jokes and rude quips about your current employer do not work.

EFFECTIVE SPEECH

The interviewers need to know:

- if you can handle the job
- if you will fit in with other staff
- how you compare to other candidates
- whether you are worth investing in.

They will find this out through detailed discussions, during which your verbal communication skills are put to the test.

GOLDEN RULE 14

Successful job seekers practise their verbal communication skills.

Be specific in your answers to questions. Give evidence, not opinions. Anybody can say, 'I'm a good communicator'. Far more impressive is the candidate who says:

> *'I've worked with staff at different levels and communicated through meetings, presentations and informal chats with all of them. I present a monthly report to the board on the department's performance, I am mentoring a new staff member in my team and I chair our weekly progress meetings.'*

Past experience can predict future performance, so sell your achievements and be prepared to explain any shortcomings. Don't rely on your personality to override any shortcomings in expertise and experience. Good interviewers are trained to avoid letting strong features of your personality influence their opinions.

It is not only *what* you say that is important but also *how* you say it. Your tone of voice, pace and non-verbal communication all contribute to the listener's response both to your words and to you as a person.

A major insurance company has developed an ideal profile for its professional trainees. Interviewers are asked to look for the following verbal skills:

- speaks fluently and uses a good range of pitch and tone to generate interest
- establishes a rapport quickly
- displays a good use of vocabulary
- listens attentively and responds accordingly.

This company understands the importance of effective speech.

Ineffective speech creates a negative impression. It can stem from a number of causes:

- speech delivered in a monotone sounds dull and can suggest that you are bored or unenthusiastic
- talking too quickly can indicate nervousness and your words will be difficult for the listener to follow and process
- loud, very slow speech can sound patronising and pompous

- mumbled, unclear delivery can suggest that you are unsure of yourself and what you are saying
- the pitch of your voice becomes higher when you are nervous. A low-pitched voice is generally thought to be more attractive.

Some people are more fluent than others. They rarely think of the way in which they speak because they don't have to. For those who are less confident, speaking is a skill that, like any other, can be improved.

Effective speech combines both verbal and non-verbal communication signals:

- modulate your tone – it should be neither too loud nor too soft
- vary the pace at which you speak
- speak clearly and avoid mumbling
- provided that the tone is varied, do not be afraid to speak more slowly than usual
- avoid slang and verbal habits such as saying 'you know' and 'like'
- don't interrupt when somebody else is speaking
- face the listener and maintain eye contact
- keep your head up because this makes your voice stronger
- take your time before you speak – don't be afraid of short pauses while you think about your response
- use hand and facial gestures when appropriate – smiling and raising or opening your hands can be used to emphasise a point without appearing aggressive.

Practise your speech

As with all skills, your ability to speak effectively will improve with practice. Your voice is a tool which you can learn to use more proficiently.

✎ Try this simple exercise. Record yourself on tape:

- reading a short extract from a newspaper
- in conversation with a friend.

However embarrassing this may be at first, persevere. As you play back the tape ask yourself:

- Can I improve my delivery?
- Am I speaking too quickly or too slowly?
- Does the tone vary according to what I am saying?
- Is the pitch pleasant to listen to or do I sound shrill?

Work on each of these aspects of your speech by recording yourself again and monitoring your progress. Try starting at a lower pitch and see if that makes an improvement. Read the newspaper extract more quickly, then more slowly. What difference does the change in pace make?

✎ Listen to competent speakers on the radio. Unlike television, radio broadcasting demands vocal skill because listeners have no visual indicators to help them understand the message. Listen to the radio news and look for ways in which the announcers use their voices. Then listen to the shipping forecast to see how a skilled speaker can make even the most repetitious information interesting!

Be assertive

We have already mentioned the importance of being assertive during the interview. You deserve as much respect as the selectors. You are asking them to consider you for a job; that will make you a colleague – and colleagues are respected. Your speech should reflect that confidence and expectation of respect.

Assertive speech involves telling people what you want to achieve without apology and without making demands. Assertive speech is unambiguous; it gives clear guidelines to the listener. In terms of the interview, assertive comments project the positive nature of your abilities without making you sound big headed.

Assertive comments use active verbs:

- 'I believe you would benefit from ...'
- 'Let me suggest ...'
- 'I am sure that I can ...'

When you are describing achievements, don't be unnecessarily modest. Again, focus on yourself:

- 'I did ...'
- 'I am working on ...'
- 'Together with my team, I am developing ...'

Avoid 'we'. It is your achievements and expertise the interviewers are considering, not the other members of your team or your current employer.

QUESTIONING TECHNIQUES

You have already considered some of the questions you may be asked – or may wish to ask yourself – during the interview. Understanding questioning techniques helps you respond more quickly when you are in the interview and will be of particular use if you take part in an assessment centre where assessors observe your communication skills.

Dialogue employs different types of questions which are usually grouped into the categories: closed, open, leading and probing questions.

Closed questions

These invite minimum feedback and interviewers use them when they want specific information. Often beginning with phrases such as:

- 'Did you ... ?'
- 'Have you ... ?'
- 'Is ... ?'
- 'Has ... ?'

Closed questions elicit a short, precise response, for example:

- 'When did you relocate to Edinburgh?'
- 'Which department will I be based in?'

Open questions

These encourage a more detailed reply. Open questions develop a dialogue and help establish a rapport. They are used to find out feelings and opinions. Open questions may begin with phrases such as:

- 'Tell me about ...'
- 'How did you ... ?'
- 'Why did you ... ?'

Leading questions

These give a strong indication of the expected answer and can exert pressure on the listener to agree. You need to be able to spot leading questions and answer them assertively. Resist the temptation to go along with the tone of the question because it may be a trick or a plant:

- 'Don't you think that psychometric tests are vastly overrated?'
- 'Wouldn't you agree that a minimum wage will push unemployment up?'

Probing questions

These use one answer as the basis for a second question, thus encouraging a deeper discussion:

- 'You say the last advertising campaign didn't meet your expectations. What particularly didn't you like about it?'

A good interviewer will use a mixture of

question styles to create a dialogue and thus a genuine exchange of information.

Handling difficult questions

However well you prepare in advance, within an interview you are likely to come up against unexpected questions. Some of these may be difficult to answer but there are techniques you can use to help you make a sensible, effective response:

- ask for clarification – repeat the question, if necessary, to make sure you and the interviewer are focusing on the same issue
- give yourself time to answer
- overcome the problem
- repeat the benefits.

Look at how this works in practice.

> **The question:**
> *'This role means that you will be leading a team of four other employees. Although you have some excellent experience in customer service, I don't see any evidence of you managing other staff.'*
>
> **Clarification:**
> *'You are concerned that I may find aspects of managing a team difficult?'*
>
> **Overcoming the problem:**
> *'My present employer is committed to team working and we all work in teams covering different functions. I've been working in the customer sales team for the last two years and have also been part of the in-store systems development team. I've learned a lot from my own team leaders – in fact, I've*

deputised for the customer services manager in his absence. We have regular briefings and team coaching sessions. I'm familiar with some of the theory behind team building and the need to bring together different types of people to get an even balance of skills and aptitudes. So although I don't have direct experience of team management, I believe it is an area I could build on.'

Repeating the benefits:
'I'm committed to team working and would welcome a chance to develop my skills as a team leader. Would there be an opportunity for training in this area?'

LISTENING SKILLS

GOLDEN RULE 15

Successful job seekers know how to listen.

A good interviewer will put you at ease and encourage you to talk. During an interview, your ability to talk fluently about your skills and experience, your direction and yourself is essential. So is your ability to listen.

Every day we are bombarded with words through conversation, television, radio. Processing all the verbal messages we receive would lead to mental overload so, as a defence mechanism, a lot of what we hear is filtered out. During an interview, that filter mechanism needs to be switched off so that you pay attention to everything that is said.

Listening skills are often neglected. In the

desire to communicate, many of us rapidly begin to dominate dialogue, without being aware of what we are doing. We know how to talk but we don't know how to listen.

> *'What gives a negative impression during an interview? A candidate who doesn't listen, doesn't pay attention and doesn't focus on the questions I'm asking but tells me what they want me to hear.'*

Listening involves far more than hearing the words. It means:

- taking in information
- processing the information
- responding to that information.

The logic is simple. The more closely you listen during the interview, the more information you receive and process. Your responses become more focused – and thus you answer the interviewer's questions more accurately and thoroughly.

Listening is a skill and, like all skills, it is something you can improve. To become an 'active listener' during an interview, it helps to understand some of the blocks to listening:

- **preoccupation** – 'I was only half listening'. You may be so preoccupied with the process of the interview and its outcome that you fail to pay real attention to what is being said. Your mind is not focused on the person you are speaking to but on other issues. Alternatively, your train of thought may be diverted by a comment somebody makes during the conversation and you find your mind wanders.

- **prediction** – 'I knew what she was going to say before she said it.' If your attention is not fully focused on what is being said, then you may predict what the other person is going to say and block out their actual words. You may assume you know what a question will be and start preparing your answer. A reason for this tendency is the speed at which people speak and listen. The average person, speaking clearly, uses 100–150 words per minute but can listen to and process up to 600 words per minute. Consequently we continue to think when somebody is speaking and anticipate their words.

- **talking** – 'Talk more, say less.' Speaking focuses attention on you therefore you may think that you have control over the interview. A fear of silence can also lead you to talk too much and dominate the conversation. The problem with this is that although words are being spoken, there is no real dialogue.

Other blocks to listening include external noises which might distract you, and difficulty in understanding language or accent.

Active listening

In an interview you should aim to exhibit active listening. Active listening shows the person with whom you are communicating that you are both hearing *and* understanding what they say. You can enhance all dialogue by using active listening skills.

- The first step to active listening is to increase your level of concentration. Focus on the speaker and do not assume you know what is coming next. Concentrate on what is being said, not what you want to say in response.
- Do not interrupt when another person is speaking, but wait until they have finished.
- Summarise the content (particularly of a long speech) to show that you understood what was said. Useful phrases include: 'So, if I've understood correctly ... ', 'As I understand it, what you are saying is ... '
- Ask questions if you need to clarify a point.
- Encourage the speaker and show that you are following the conversation by nodding and agreeing when appropriate.
- Use continuity noises such as 'mm', 'ahha', 'yes', etc.
- Face the speaker.
- Lean forward rather than back to indicate that you are paying attention.
- Maintain eye contact.

Never be afraid to say that you have not heard or understood a question and ask for it to be repeated. Similiarly, if an interviewer uses a term you haven't heard before, ask them to explain. It can save embarrassment later.

'One of my students came back from an interview and asked what remuneration was. When I told her, she burst into tears. The interviewer had asked what remuneration she

expected and, because she had no idea what the word meant, she made a wild guess. She told him she wanted to make a career in retailing and hoped one day to run her own department.'

Practise listening

Becoming a good, responsive listener takes practice. If you think your listening skills need improving then try a couple of listening activities.

- Listen to and simultaneously tape a radio programme for five minutes. Wait fifteen minutes, then write down as much as you can remember of what you heard. Focus not on the actual words, but the essence of the broadcast. Play back the tape and compare it to your notes. How accurate were you?

- During a conversation, ask a friend to monitor your listening skills. Do you show signs of being an active listener? Ask them to check:

- whether you remain focused on them when they are speaking
- non-verbal signals, such as eye contacts and posture
- whether you interrupt
- the quality of your response to what they are saying – do they feel that you are really listening?

NON-VERBAL COMMUNICATION

> **GOLDEN RULE 16**
>
> Successful job seekers understand the basics of non-verbal communication.

The same insurance company which specified verbal skills for new recruits also identified the following desirable non-verbal communication skills:

- body language is positive and confident
- body language conveys a businesslike image.

There is non-verbal communication whenever you are with another person. It is impossible *not* to send out messages, therefore it is important to be aware of what these messages convey. However, although it may help you within an interview to understand some of the principles of non-verbal communication, too much attention to this can detract from the interview as a whole. If you are spending all your time and energy watching your interviewer to pick up hints as to what they are thinking, you will not be concentrating fully on their words.

It is important, therefore, to consider non-verbal communication as complementary to the spoken word in helping to get messages across from one person to another.

The term 'body language' is often used instead of 'non-verbal communication'. It is inaccurate in that non-verbal communication covers much more than physical movement.

Messages are communicated by your:

- posture
- gestures
- expression
- movement
- tone of voice
- dress and appearance
- distance from other people.

In an interview, you are sending messages to the interviewer by the way you:

- enter the room
- stand
- sit
- use hand gestures
- use eye movements
- use facial expression
- dress.

Examples of negative postures include:

- slouching in your chair – too casual and unconcerned
- folded arms – defensive, self-protective
- clenching your fists
- crossing your legs and swinging your foot – distracting
- brushing back your hair – a sign that you are nervous.

Positive postures include:

- sitting upright with your shoulders back
- maintaining eye contact
- a relaxed posture with hands unclenched
- smiling
- hand movements with the palm held upwards.

Some psychologists suggest that non-verbal communication stems from our subconscious so it reflects our true feelings more accurately than the words we speak. We think about our words and make a conscious decision whether or not to speak them, therefore we are continually editing our thoughts. Non-verbal communication is far less controlled so arguably it gives a more genuine message.

Beware of misreading non-verbal communication

It follows that by paying greater attention to non-verbal communication we can decode the subtext of a conversation and find out what somebody is really thinking. However, there are certain caveats to that assumption. For example, you may be talking to somebody who is particularly adept at using non-verbal communication. Customer service staff are often trained to hide their true thoughts and emotions and to use positive non-verbal communication at all times.

Secondly, how non-verbal communication is interpreted may vary according to culture. Pointing with the forefinger is offensive in some South East Asian cultures but a normal, everyday gesture in Europe. A smile from an Asian colleague may indicate pleasure – but equally could suggest extreme embarrassment. So your interpretation of non-verbal communication must take cultural values into consideration.

Thirdly, we all have personal idiosyncrasies, gestures of which we may scarcely be aware. A person who continually pushes their hair away from their face may be nervous – equally this could be a habit established since childhood. Also, recognise that physical factors such as disability or incapacity can affect the way somebody stands, sits or moves around.

Finally, although awareness of body language is helpful, don't let it overcomplicate your reactions. A person who folds their arms may simply be cold rather than displaying a defence mechanism!

> 'I've become very conscious of the way I present myself during an interview. I'm careful to avoid fidgeting and touching my face, and I try to keep eye contact with the interviewer. It's not always easy because some things you do without thinking like folding your arms. My particular habit was to keep pushing my hair away from my forehead. I got friends to tell me every time I did it – and gradually stopped.'

Common non-verbal signs

This chart indicates some of the commonly accepted interpretations of non-verbal communication which you may come across in an interview situation.

Nervous:

- fidgeting
- nail biting and picking at fingers
- tugging earlobes, playing with hair
- covering mouth with hand
- interrupting

Confident:

- standing or sitting erect
- maintaining eye contact
- leaning forward in one's seat
- smiling

Bored:

- drumming fingers
- tapping feet
- doodling
- fidgeting
- lack of eye contact
- supporting head on hands

Interested:

- raised or tilted head
- elbows on table, fingers forming a steeple

Aggressive:

- pointing
- breathing quickly
- banging on the table
- legs crossed with ankle on supporting knee
- interrupting

Defensive:

- arms folded tightly across chest
- legs crossed
- gripping arms of chair
- hands clenched
- lack of eye contact
- head down or averted
- touching one's face

CLOSING THE INTERVIEW

At the end of the interview, you should be clear about what happens next. If you are not, then ask:

- Will the organisation notify applicants of their decision – by telephone or in writing?
- When will that decision be made?
- When do they anticipate the successful applicant will start work?
- Do they require you to send any supporting information or documentation such as certificates, etc.?
- When will they approach referees?

At the end of the interview, thank the interviewer or the members of the panel. If you have enjoyed the time you spent in the interview room – or at least found it more enlightening and pleasant than you anticipated – then say so.

AFTER THE INTERVIEW

As soon as possible after the interview, take half an hour to make a note of how you think it went. Which questions did you answer well? Were there any parts that you found difficult? If so, how can you prepare for similar situations in future interviews?

Make a note of all the people with whom you spoke, and the key dates for decisions and notification. If you haven't heard anything after that date, contact the company again. Keep these notes with your personal databank so that you have a clear record of your progress.

SUMMARY

In Part Three of *Job Seeking* you have looked at the steps you can take to prepare for the interview and to improve your interview skills. You should now be aware that careful preparation can help to combat 'interview nerves' and help you present a more polished, professional image to the interviewer.

As we said when you were preparing for the interview, this advice may appear lengthy and detailed but much of what is suggested will already be second nature to you. Above all, be yourself. Creating the wrong impression, even if it gets you the job, leaves you in a difficult position. When you start work, you will be suppressing parts of your personality. How long can you keep that up? If by nature you are energetic, outgoing and effervescent, what is the point of presenting yourself as a sober, restrained individual who prefers to take a back seat? Yes, you may get the job if that is the sort of person they are looking for – but will you be happy there? And when your natural ebullience shows through, will *they* be happy with *you*?

If, despite your planning, an interview does not go as well as you anticipated, don't be too hard on yourself. The interviewer's perception of your performance may be different from your own. Use each interview as a learning exercise, not as an excuse for self-criticism.

After the interview, you will wait for the organisation's decision. This can be a difficult time – although if you are a serious job seeker involved in a systematic job search, you will have little time to dwell on the outcome of one interview. You will still be looking for, and responding to, other vacancies.

In Part Four you will consider what happens after the selectors' decision has been made.

Part four
STEPPING BACK

GOLDEN RULE 17

Successful job seekers do not make snap decisions.

What happens after the interview?

- You are offered the job you want, stop job seeking and start celebrating.
- You are offered a job but you are no longer sure it is the job you want.
- Your job search has been so successful that you are offered more than one job and must make a choice.
- You are not offered the job, so you continue the job search using the experiences you have gained so far to improve your performance.

Unless the outcome was the first of these possibilities, the final stage of the job search is not straightforward. It demands that you make decisions that will affect your professional future. A knee-jerk reaction could result in you accepting a position, or a deal, that you do not really want.

If you have to choose between two vacancies (and it *does* happen) how do you decide which is the right one for you? And if you have been unsuccessful and received a letter of rejection, how do you remain positive and keep searching?

Part Four of *Job Seeking* looks at evaluating job offers, negotiating deals and getting feedback.

EVALUATING A JOB OFFER

'Something happened that, at the beginning of my job search, I hadn't anticipated. I received offers from two companies within two days. They were both for positions that held a lot of responsibility, both with companies that were at the cutting edge of their sector. Making a decision about which one to choose was one of the hardest tasks I've ever done. At times I was tempted to toss a coin and make my mind up according to which way it fell.'

This applicant was fortunate but if you have planned and operated a systematic and thorough job search campaign this is a situation you need to plan for. If you are sending out applications and attending interviews on a regular basis, there is every chance that you will be offered more than one job.

However many job offers you receive – one or a dozen – you still need to evaluate each one to decide if it is the right opportunity for you. If you accept a position that is not suitable, you could find yourself trapped in employment that you do not enjoy and starting the job search all over again.

Evaluating a job offer involves finding out as much as you can about:

- the working environment
- contractual details.

As you worked through the written application and interview procedures, you built up a fair picture of what the work involves. You will also have found out something about the organisation, its culture, philosophy and management practices.

The working environment

Add to this factual information the impressions you gained when you visited the company for interview or during site orientation. Did you like the location and set-up of the workplace? Did you feel that this was a working environment in which you could thrive? What did you think of the other staff? Think about everyone you met, from the receptionists through to senior management. Did they appear purposeful, committed, pleased to be there? Is this a company where colleagues appear to work in harmony – or did you find evidence of disquiet and frustration?

Depending on your own personality and attitude to work, these factors may be of major importance or rather insignificant. If, as a technical officer, you spend large parts of your day working alone in a laboratory developing your own projects, you may be oblivious to your surroundings. On the other hand, if your job involves constant contact with other team members, working in an open plan environment and spending the bulk of your time in meetings with other staff, staff morale and attitude are critical to your own success.

Practicalities

Don't underestimate the importance of what seem to be minor concerns. For example, the distance between your home and work can make a huge difference to your life. At interview, commuting may seem a small price to pay for getting the job – but it can be a major drain on both your energy level and bank balance.

Ask yourself:

- How long did it take you to get to the company when you attended the interview?
- Will your job involve a long journey?
- If so, how much will this cost you in both time and money?

If you are already used to commuting and see it as part of your working life, this will not be a problem. If, on the other hand, you have always worked close to home, commuting can be hard to come to terms with.

'My employer is based in Leeds and my home is about thirty miles away. There were a couple of through trains in the morning and evening. I saw it as a chance to catch up on extra work, read the newspaper and relax for fifty minutes. The first couple of months were OK, but I found it stressful to have to be at the station for a fixed time every day – and to know that if I missed my train there wasn't another one. Plus, as winter set in, there were frequent delays and disruptions to the service and I always seemed to be in a hurry. After a while I started driving to work. Although the first part of the journey took very little time, once I reached the outskirts of the city I was stuck in traffic for at least half an hour. Commuting added an extra two – sometimes three – hours to the working day. I hated the travelling and at weekends spent most of my time asleep because I was so

tired. And it cost me a fortune in train fares or petrol. I would probably have saved money by working for a lower salary nearer to home.'

Other practical considerations you need to think about before you take the job are:

- the amount of travelling (in addition to commuting) your job will involve. How will periods away from home impact on your family and home life?

- the possibility of relocation – is your future employer likely to relocate? Do you have to commit to being mobile and possibly move to other parts of the country?

Contractual details

The contract of employment between you and your employer sets out obligations on both sides. Consequently, it is desirable to see the contract *before* you accept the job. That may not be possible as some companies will not produce an employment contract until some weeks after you start work. Nevertheless, understanding what the contract contains provides you with a list of the information you need to evaluate the job offer and to decide whether you want the job. Determining these criteria can save misunderstanding and problems at a later date.

Employers should, at your request, be able to show you a draft contract. Don't be afraid to ask to see this – you are showing a thorough, professional approach in wanting to gather as much detail as possible before you make a decision. Your thoroughness also helps the employer to clarify what is on offer and what you are anticipating in the job. It is in their interests to recruit and select employees who are happy with their situation and committed to staying. If you have any doubts about the terms and conditions, don't accept the position until these have been resolved.

> 'At the final interview I was given details of salary, bonuses and holiday entitlement. It seemed a fair package and I was very keen to take the job. I remember being told that my starting salary would be reviewed after six months' employment with the company. As the end of the six months approached, I began to anticipate the review. My boss said nothing and I didn't have the confidence to bring up the subject. Finally I talked in confidence to one of my colleagues. She was amused – it seems that we were all promised a six month review but it never materialised. And of course, there was nothing in my contract of employment.'

This list shows what a typical contract includes. These are all points that you should be clear on before accepting the job:

- employer's name (make sure you know which part of the company is employing you if it is part of a group)
- your job title
- date your employment starts (this is important if your salary is reviewed annually on the anniversary of your starting date)
- salary amount and date when it is paid
- holiday entitlement

- sickness provision
- pension scheme
- hours and place of work
- discipline and complaints procedures
- notice periods for both sides.

These details, once incorporated in the contract, cannot be altered unless you are given notice that your employment conditions are going to change. In some countries, employees can reject proposed changes if they think that they are unfair – for example, if hours are substantially increased or holiday entitlements cut.

There are other salary and benefit issues that you need to discuss before committing to the job:

- dates at which salary is reviewed
- targets and how these affect earnings
- commission and bonuses, including frequency of payments
- share options
- expense account entitlement and procedure
- travel subsidies such as season ticket loans
- company car and the basis on which it is allocated, rules on private mileage, replacement policy, option to buy, etc.
- private healthcare.

You may also want to discuss the following if they apply to your particular situation:

- the appraisal system
- maternity leave and childcare provision
- development opportunities, particularly if the company is willing to sponsor study programmes
- provision for flexible working such as flexitime, annualised hours, working from

home and job sharing
- relocation expenses and package
- trade union membership.

This is an extensive list to work through with your prospective employer but you need as much information as possible if you are to make a fair evaluation of the job offer. Employers should have most of this information to hand and be pleased to discuss it with you.

TIMING

Once you have gathered all the information relevant to your decision, you may know exactly which way you want to go. If you are not sure, then ask for time to consider and set a firm date when you will get back to the company with your decision. Obviously, this cannot be too long since the human resources function may be under pressure to get a new recruit in place, but it is reasonable to ask for up to a week.

Make sure that you have a named contact to whom you can speak in the interim period if you need further clarification on the terms you have discussed.

Of course, there are situations where you will be expected to make a speedy decision. If this happens to you but you feel that the employer has not provided sufficient information about conditions and benefits, ask yourself: How much do I want this position?

Only you know the answer to that question.

MAKING THE DECISION

Go back to the notes you made as you read through Part One. How much does this offer match your ideal job? How far will you be compromising if you accept?

Discuss your decision with those who will be affected by it, such as your partner, spouse or family members. Your job impacts on those closest to you not only in the practical terms of providing an income but also in the way it affects your state of mind. Will this job give you the satisfaction you need? If so – go for it.

If you have a friend who acts as an unofficial mentor then consult him or her, but don't expect anybody else to make the decision for you.

There is a lot to be said for the traditional method of writing down the pros and cons of a new job in two columns, but to do this successfully you must be absolutely honest about what it offers you.

Don't be rushed into making a decision. If you have doubts, don't be afraid to voice them. You have got this far, which suggests that other opportunities will come your way.

NEGOTIATING SKILLS

> **GOLDEN RULE 18**
>
> Successful job seekers negotiate the deal they want.

You may be offered a job where the salary and benefits package is fixed, in which case you will not need to negotiate with your employers. Even so, understanding the basics of negotiation can still prove useful. In months to come, you may be in a position to renegotiate your package and at that point you will use your negotiating skills.

How much are you worth?

A number of factors influence salary offers:

- **the industry norm for your type of work**. In some professions such as teaching, local government and the Civil Service, this will be fixed according to pay scales. In other areas of employment, the salary will fall into a range or bracket or could be negotiated according to your experience.

- **your location**. A recent advertisement for a copywriter in North Yorkshire offered a salary of only £10,000. Someone taking the same level of responsibility in an urban area might anticipate considerably more. Expect a higher rate of pay in London or an additional payment

(London Weighting) to compensate for the cost of living.

- **your qualifications and experience**. A graduate recruit will command a higher starting salary than a non-graduate. In some companies, graduate salaries vary according to the level of the degree, with a person with a first-class honours receiving more than someone with an upper second. Your experience will also be a consideration – your salary may reflect the years you have spent in your particular career.

- **recent performance**. If you can give evidence of outstanding performance in your current or last job, then your new employer may be willing to invest more in getting you into the company.

- **your rarity value**. If you have a talent, technical or professional skill that is in short supply, then your value goes up.

- **your perceived worth to the employer**. In other words, your ability to generate profits and improve the organisation's service.

Before negotiations start

If your salary is negotiable, try to avoid detailed discussions until you have been offered the job. During your interview, state that this is not a major priority at this point although you will want to discuss it later. Thus, when you come to negotiate salary, you already know that the employer wants you.

You will also have gained some time to research salary levels.

Although you may not be able to predict exactly what the employer is willing to pay, researching salary levels before you start negotiations can take you a long way down the road towards getting an acceptable offer. There are some points you can clarify, such as the going rate for jobs where you live, by:

- checking the local press for comparable jobs
- checking professional journals
- checking Internet recruitment sites for salary ranges in your profession across the country
- checking starting rates in your profession. If a graduate recruit to a management trainee programme with a high street retailer starts on £18,000 per year, how much can you, a manager with five years' experience, expect to be paid?

You may be in a position to talk to colleagues in the same type of employment (or even within the same company) to get an idea of the offers that are currently being put on the table. However, in this country salary remains a topic which many people prefer not to discuss, so you may find friends and colleagues avoid giving precise information.

Set your limits

Negotiation involves reaching a compromise that is acceptable to both parties. Before you start negotiations, identify a realistic figure or package that you can accept. Ask yourself:

- How much do I think this job is worth? Take into consideration not only the salary and benefits package, but the level of responsibility you will be taking on, your promotion prospects, etc. This is your target figure.

- What is the absolute minimum I will accept? This is your base line.

When you negotiate, the further you move below the target figure, the more you should ask yourself if this is really the job you want. Under no circumstances should you go below the base line. Accepting a package that is a long way below your expectations may cause resentment later.

> 'At the time, I remember thinking that the salary offer was on the low side but it didn't seem to matter because I was so pleased to be offered the job. Months later, when the honeymoon period was over, it became a real source of irritation. I was working long hours, pulling in a lot of new business and felt that I wasn't being paid what I was worth. It is hard to be objective in these situations. The resentment builds up and you want to punish your employer in some way by working less or making it clear that you are unhappy, both of which were unacceptable reactions. I made a commitment when I accepted the job to take what was offered. It wasn't my employer's fault that I was now dissatisfied.'

What can you trade?

Identify areas where you are willing to compromise. This gives both you and the employer a degree of flexibility – but do not go below your base line.

For example, you may agree to trade:

- a lower salary for a company car
- longer hours for an above average holiday allowance
- a reduced bonus for a higher basic salary.

Go back to Part One and consider what you were originally looking for in a new job. Are you still on course to achieve your aims?

Prepare your arguments

Why should your new employer give you what you want? If the initial offer is low, then it is up to you to convince them that you are worth more. Collect all the relevant information before you start negotiating; you may find it useful to put this in writing for your own reference or to show to the employer. Useful arguments include:

- evidence of pay and conditions for similar work
- a review of what you are bringing to the organisation.

How you deliver these points is important. Avoid trying to shame or bully the employer into offering you a better deal by making scathing comparisons. Negotiation is about compromise, not confrontation.

Think positive

This employer has offered you a job. The organisation not only wants you, they need your services. They should therefore be willing to pay a fair rate for these services. How you perceive yourself during negotiations will influence your future employer's perceptions. Don't undersell yourself and be assertive.

Remember what we said about assertive behaviour in Part Three (page 136). Consider the ways in which you can communicate your positive attitude through speech and non-verbal communication.

Opening negotiations

The opening stages of negotiations involve establishing a relationship and finding out where you both stand. You need to communicate *your* expectations and get some idea of *their* expectations. Remember to:

- move slowly – it may take some time to achieve a final decision that is acceptable to both parties

- avoid laying down ultimatums – 'I won't accept less than £xxx.' This will restrict your options. You need room to manoeuvre. Also avoid implied threats that if you don't get what you want, you will take your ball away. If you hint that another company is offering a better deal, you could be told to take it

- take the initiative by asking them to make the opening offer. The company will already have a salary and benefits package in mind so you want their offer in the open before you indicate your expectations

Assertive	Aggressive	Passive
You both win	You win, they lose	You lose, they win
Body language • steady eye contact • head up, hands relaxed	**Body language** • staring • tight body language, pointing, thumping the table	**Body language** • evasive eye contact • crossed arms, pressing well back in your seat, smiling nervously
Steady, calm, modulated voice	Harsh, loud, abrupt speech	Hesitant, low or inaudible speech, apologising
Verbal communication • 'I think we could meet halfway' • 'We can work together'	**Verbal communication** • 'That's not acceptable' • 'I can't accept that'	**Verbal communication** • 'Yes, please, if that's what you want' • 'I don't mind'

- when that offer is made, remain calm. If it is more than you anticipated, don't be overenthusiastic. The company has made an initial offer and will be expecting you to use this as a basis for further discussion. If the offer is much lower than you expected, try not to show your disappointment or be drawn into making statements that give you away. You can negotiate to improve a low offer. You can do nothing if you say, 'That's ridiculous,' and walk out of the interview

- take note of both verbal and non-verbal communication indicators. They help you to see how the negotiations are progressing and stop you from pushing too hard.

Bargaining strategies

This stage of the negotiation process lets you get more information and test the flexibility of the employer. Both sides put forward suggestions to test the response of the other party:

- avoid making demands, because these can be refused

- be aware of the whole benefits package and don't allow the negotiations to concentrate on any one area for too long. Keep thinking back to your target

- make provisional offers so that both sides feel that they are gaining: 'I may be able to accept that salary if you can offer a company car.'

- present any evidence you have collected

to support your expectations. This will be based on your knowledge of the job market gained through research before the negotiations begin

- reassure your new employer that you are not being adversarial. Make it clear that you are looking for a compromise because you both want an acceptable outcome.

Key bargaining phrases

- 'If I could … could you … ?'
- 'I had hoped for … but I would accept … '
- 'I would be willing to … if you could … '
- 'I wouldn't usually consider … but in this case … '

Note how a balance is maintained throughout the dialogue between what both parties can offer. You are offering to reach a compromise. Your offers can, however, be structured to gain exactly what you want.

Closing the negotiations

The final stages of negotiation should bring an agreement that is acceptable to both sides:

- make sure that both you and the employer are clear on what has been agreed by summarising the deal. Ask for written confirmation of the offer

- accept that you negotiated the deal, that you had control throughout the process. You should therefore be happy with what you have achieved and should not come out of the negotiations wondering if you could have gained more

- if you do leave feeling disappointed or in any way aggrieved, this suggests that the negotiation has not been successful for you. Can you really accept what is on offer?

FEEDBACK

> **GOLDEN RULE 19**
>
> Successful job seekers value feedback.

So far in Part Four we have dealt with positive outcomes and assumed that you have been offered the job you wanted. But if you receive the plain white envelope containing the polite refusal, what happens next?

Facing rejection is always difficult and it would be glib to suggest that there is a way to ease the initial sense of resentment, anger or disillusion. You have worked hard to get to the interview stage and may well have built up your hopes that this job was *the one* – only to be told that your services are not required.

To ignore your frustration at receiving a refusal doesn't help. You need to allow room for your disappointment. Whether that takes a couple of minutes or a couple of days, it must be faced. Only then can you move forward.

> *'Of course it's frustrating to get a rejection and of course you feel a bit hurt. But the more jobs I applied for, the less the refusals affected me. I felt more in control because I*

was looking at a range of vacancies, all of which attracted me. If one employer didn't come through, maybe the next one would. So I started actually reading the letters and looking for tips rather than just taking in the first sentence and throwing them away.'

If you are following a systematic job search, a rejection is just one stage in an ongoing process. You will be continually identifying vacancies, continually writing applications and receiving invitations to interview. A rejection letter marks the end of one application but, if you have followed the advice in this book and maintained a regular and organised job search there will be other applications in the pipeline. Now you must focus on these.

Before you file the rejection letter away – or throw it in the bin – ask yourself if you can use it in some way to improve your chances with the next application. Read through it again. What does it tell you? It may be a personal response which gives you some idea of how you performed and why you didn't get the job. More likely it will be the standard '... due to the very high quality of applicants ... we regret that on this occasion ... '.

Is this really enough? What you need is feedback and positive advice.

Feedback gives us information about how our behaviour is perceived by others. It helps us to understand:

- what we are doing
- how well we are performing
- how our behaviour affects other people.

Why feedback is useful

A meeting with one of the interviewers, or a contact within the organisation who has been involved with your application, will help you:

- find out which aspects of your experience and expertise (as shown in your CV or application form) attracted the attention of the recruiters
- understand what you did well in the interview
- identify areas in which you could improve your performance
- pick up tips on what selectors look for in a good candidate
- make decisions about how you need to amend or change your approach.

Getting feedback is an essential part of working life. When you study, you expect your assignments to be marked and commented upon – that's feedback. When colleagues report back to you on a new venture or your department's sales performance – that's feedback. Written reports and company accounts, appraisals, informal discussions – they all give you feedback.

Feedback helps you to understand what you are doing well and what you need to improve upon. It is an important indicator of your progress and can highlight new directions. Yet when it comes to the job search, many people avoid getting feedback. That particular part of the search is over, that potential avenue for employment has proved to be a dead end. They turned you down for the job and the last thing you want to do is get in touch with the organisation again. What is the point of discussing why they chose somebody else for a post you really wanted?

To take such a negative view of the feedback process is to cut off a valuable source of information and intelligence that could mean the difference between succeeding and failing in your next application.

Asking for feedback

Asking for feedback is not the same as asking why you didn't get the job. It is a means of learning more about what employers are looking for so that you can improve your technique and performance in future interviews.

Being able to seek and receive feedback about your performance are valuable skills and, like all skills, they can be improved and enhanced. The main barrier to getting constructive feedback will be your own attitude. Fear that you will hear comments that will dent your confidence, or that you will inconvenience or embarrass the interviewer may prevent you taking part in a meeting that can help your performance.

> *'I consider giving feedback to be a key part of my job. It can help candidates and it often helps me to identify how well our recruitment and selection processes are working. What amazes me is how few applicants actually call me and ask to discuss their applications.'*

Ringing up an employer on the spur of the moment and demanding 'Why didn't I get the job, then?' won't get you very far. Plan your tactics for getting and receiving feedback in the same way you planned every stage of your job search. The important points to consider are:

- timing
- making contact
- preparation
- staying objective
- staying positive
- being alert
- active listening.

Timing

Try to set in motion the process for getting feedback as soon as you receive a decision about the job. Contact the interviewer or the human resources manager by telephone while your interview is fresh in their memory.

Making contact

Try to see your contact face-to-face – or at least arrange a time when you can have a fairly lengthy discussion over the telephone. Avoid relying on written feedback because you may simply get a standard letter. Ring to make an appointment and be reasonably persistent. An experienced interviewer will understand why you want feedback and be willing to help.

Give them a few days to prepare for the meeting. They will have moved on to other tasks so be prepared to wait for a date and time when it is convenient for you both to meet.

Preparation

Before you make the first telephone call to

your contact, decide what you want from them. Focus on key issues and don't try to cover too many areas in one short meeting.

Plan your questions. You want feedback on:

- your CV or application form
- your covering letter
- your interview technique.

You may also want to find out more about opportunities in your job area and to discuss what this particular employer was looking for.

Give the interviewer precise areas on which to focus. In this situation, *you* can set the agenda and determine the direction of the discussion.

Prepare using open questions so that you will get full answers. Ask: how?, what?, why? Keep the tone positive. Rather than asking, 'Do you have any comments about my CV', ask 'Can you suggest ways in which I can improve my CV?'

Useful – and encouraging – phrases to get more information from your contact include:

- 'What exactly would you suggest?'
- 'Can you give me an example?'
- 'What areas are you thinking of?'
- 'How do you think I could ... ?'

Staying objective

Focus on facts and stick to your objectives as the discussion progresses. Take notes, if it helps. Don't get sidetracked by taking comments as a reflection on your personality. It is not your personality that you want to discuss, it is your job-seeking skills. Keep the emphasis on how you can improve.

Discussing the job market in your profession can be very useful, particularly if you are talking to HR professionals. They may have information about other companies in your region and they should be able to point towards training and development opportunities that will be useful to you as you continue your job search.

Staying positive

If you feel resentful, frustrated or angry that you didn't get the job, your emotions will show however hard you try to hide them. Remember that your purpose is to improve your performance. This particular company may not have offered you the job but the next one might.

Being alert

Watch the interviewer's non-verbal communication indicators and listen to their tone of voice so you know when they have said everything they can. That's when you say thank you and leave.

If the interviewer starts to:

- shuffle papers
- sound pressured or irritated
- lose the thread of the conversation and move away from the main point
- use defensive body language such as averting their eyes, folding their arms, tapping their fingers

then you are receiving signals that your time is up!

Watch yourself. If you:

- start to interrupt
- want to disagree or interject with 'but'
- start to frown or scowl

- want to reject what is being said
- lose concentration
- justify yourself with comments like 'What I meant was ... ,' or 'I wasn't given the chance to ... '

then you are no longer getting anything useful from the conversation. It's time for you to make a graceful exit.

Active listening

Use your listening skills. You may find it useful to refer back to the section on listening skills before your feedback meeting.

Ask a question and listen to what is being said, not what you think is being said. If you are not clear on a response, ask for more detail.

Finally, whether you agree with everything that has been said or not, show your appreciation of the time the interviewer has taken to talk to you. Thank them and send a brief note a couple of days later reiterating how useful the process has been.

Why? Because if you got this far, you want to be remembered in the best possible way. This interviewer could be recruiting again in the future. They may also know of other vacancies that could be suitable for you.

> 'Two days after I received the letter saying I hadn't got the job, I phoned the human resources manager. It wasn't a call I enjoyed making – part of me wanted to write the whole application off and forget about it. I thought it might be a bit embarrassing for the HR manager to talk to me. Her letter was polite enough but I didn't think she'd want to waste time on someone who was now out of

the picture. I was totally wrong. She was very friendly and suggested that I come in and see her for half an hour.

'We looked through my CV again and in the light of comments I'd made at the interview, she suggested ways in which I could reorganise the information to highlight relevant skills and experience. We talked about the interview and she said that although I'd obviously been quite nervous, I'd performed well. She thought a little more preparation might have helped – for example, I could have thought about how I would answer fairly standard questions such as describing what I had to offer the company and how I saw my career path developing. Finally she explained just how high the standard of applications had been and that I was one of only four selected for interview out of more than 50 applicants.

'I came out of the meeting feeling a lot better about myself and my chances of finding the right job. That was probably the most important result of the meeting. But I also used her advice and spent some time improving my CV and planning for future interviews.'

Recording the feedback

Straight after the meeting, prepare a feedback report to record as much of what was said as possible. Use the following headings as a guide.

FEEDBACK REPORT

Vacancy

Organisation

Contact

Feedback approach – telephone (date)

Feedback approach – meeting (date)

Follow-up letter (date)

Feedback comments

CV

Application form

Covering letter

Interview skills

Fill in the report immediately – then wait for a couple of days before you sit down and reflect on what you have learned. Give yourself time to put the interview and the feedback comments into perspective, then evaluate the responses.

- Can you see any ways in which you should restructure or change your CV?
- How do the feedback comments help you to prepare for your next interview?

KEEPING RECORDS

In Part One you wrote down what you were looking for in your ideal job. In Part Two, you compiled a personal databank to keep an up-to-date record of all your experience and achievements. As your job search progresses, you should also add details of any contacts you make, CVs and application forms you send out and interviews you attend. Finally, include any feedback comments.

Keep all this information together in a format where it is easily accessible. To keep track of all your applications, you need a written record of the following:

APPLICATION RECORD

Name of organisation

Name of contact

Source of initial contact (advertisement, speculative letter, etc.)

Date of initial contact

Response

Follow-up telephone contact

Date of interview/meeting

Date of follow-up letter

Date of feedback meeting

How you store this information (and the contents of your databank) is up to you. Many people set up directories on their PC, others prefer to use index cards. The most important factor is that the information is easily accessible and you can look at it every couple of days.

Keeping records serves a number of purposes. First, it helps you to keep a check on who you have approached and what stage of the application you have reached. Every application includes different stages and, if you are following up a number of leads, it is easy to overlook steps that you should take.

Secondly, keeping a clear record will keep you on track. As a serious job seeker, you will be making a lot of approaches and you must keep submitting those applications to prospective employers. Your records will highlight times when you are slowing down. They will also help you to spot avenues that you are not exploring fully. For example, when you look back are you relying too heavily on finding vacancies from only one source? Are you using your network and sending out plenty of speculative letters?

Thirdly, recording the progress of your job search can give you a psychological boost. It shows just how much you are doing and the progress you are making. Stay positive. Remember that the more applications you make, the wider you cast your net, the more chance you have of finding the job you want.

SUMMARY

In Part Four you looked at the final stages of the job search – and took a step back to consider whether you were accepting a job you really wanted. This included examining the salary and benefits package your new employer was offering and polishing up your negotiating skills.

For those candidates who are unsuccessful with a particular application, the importance of getting feedback cannot be over-emphasised. It is one of the keys to your success in the future.

A reminder to keep accurate records brings you to the end of *Job Seeking*. Hopefully this book has helped you both to organise and structure your job search and to improve your job-seeking skills.

CONCLUSION

Interviewing different people to prepare this book was a fascinating exercise. We have all been job seekers at some time during our careers so everybody had plenty of advice to offer. Most of it was very useful. No two people had exactly the same approach to job seeking, no two organisations recruited and selected staff in exactly the same way – but all had something positive to contribute.

What rapidly became evident was a change in attitude towards job seeking. Some people still approach the task with trepidation but many others see it as a challenge. Looking for new employment is not automatically the result of a bad experience with one's present employer. For a growing section of the population it is a valid means of achieving career progress.

Many organisations accept that the modern workforce demands a degree of mobility. Some companies attempt to provide this by offering greater opportunities internally and they have implemented efficient appraisal systems to ensure staff are constantly developing their careers. But as one human resources manager said: 'These days, people move around a lot more than they did fifteen or twenty years ago. I think the desire for change goes much deeper than the pursuit of a better job. We are experiencing a culture change that is reflected in the employment market.'

As the culture of 'a job for life' recedes, then mastering job-seeking skills becomes ever more important.

Here are some final comments:

> 'As I've moved further in my career, I've become more confident about looking for what I want. Work is such a major part of my life that I owe it to myself to find a job that I really enjoy. If that means moving every four or five years, then so be it.'

> 'I defy anyone not to feel some degree of nervousness before they walk into an interview. But you can help yourself to stay in control – and I think that's what employers want to see.'

> 'We place a lot of emphasis on finding the right candidate for the job. An unhappy member of staff is unproductive and is a disruptive force within the organisation. I think it's up to us to make sure we find the person who will be happy here, so we have fairly detailed recruitment and selection processes. That's not because we are judging people but because we are looking for the best fit.'

> 'Once I started looking at applying for jobs as a challenge, it was much easier. I didn't feel so desperate any more and I paid much more attention to looking at the company to see if I wanted to work for them.'

> 'Looking for a job used all the skills I practise every day at work – communication skills, organisation skills, research skills. I'd just never thought about it like that before.'

The job-seeking process is not easy but you can help yourself to improve your chances of success. As this book has shown, your willingness to work at the job search, to put effort into improving your skills and to devote time and effort to finding and following up opportunities is paramount. Prepare every step of the way, don't give up if things don't always go the way you want them to go, and believe in yourself.

Which brings us to the final rule:

GOLDEN RULE 20

Successful job seekers never stop looking, never stop preparing and never stop following up leads.

Your job is out there. Now go out and get it!

THE GOLDEN RULES

1. **Successful job seekers know why they are looking for a new job.** There is a big difference between waking up on Monday morning feeling vaguely discontented about going to work and genuinely wanting to find a new position with another employer. Spend some time analysing what you want from your career. Will changing your job help you to achieve your goals?

2. **Successful job seekers gain an advantage by understanding the recruitment and selection processes.** Being aware of the systems and methods organisations use to find and select staff will help you target your job search and approach new companies with greater confidence.

3. **Successful job seekers know where to look for suitable vacancies.** Statistically, responding to advertisements is one of the least successful ways of finding a new job. Broaden your search by networking, using recruitment consultants and making direct approaches to companies in which you are interested.

4. **Successful job seekers tailor every approach to meet the needs of the employer.** No two jobs are the same and your applications should reflect this. Look for indicators of what the employer wants and then consider your own credentials. How can you show

5. **Successful job seekers spend time on correspondence.** Letters, CVs and application forms are your first contact with an organisation, so they must impress. Think about what you want to say, plan, draft and redraft. The old rules hold firm. All your correspondence should be pristine, carefully checked and pleasing to look at.

6. **Successful job seekers have more than one CV.** Depending on the vacancy and what the employer is looking for, it may be appropriate to send a functional, chronological or experience-based CV. Don't assume that you can mail out the same CV every time you make an application. Read the job description and tailor your CV to meet the employer's needs.

7. **Successful job seekers understand how application forms work.** Consequently they are skilled at incorporating a large volume of information in a few words. Read the application form, determine what the employer really wants to know, then draft your answers before you start filling in the boxes.

8. **Successful job seekers use covering letters to create impact.** Your covering letter which accompanies your CV or application form is your personal direct marketing campaign. It must be strong enough to make you stand out from other applicants. It takes practice to

create an impression on one page of A4 paper, but it can be done. Be brief and make sure that what you write relates to the organisation's needs.

9. **Successful job seekers prepare before they pick up the phone.** The telephone can be a great ally during the job search. It helps you gain information, make contact and establish a rapport with potential employers. To speak confidently and assertively on the phone you should identify what you want to achieve before you pick up the receiver. A few minutes spent preparing yourself for the call will help you to control the conversation so you get the result you want.

10. **Successful job seekers prepare thoroughly before the interview.** Would you sit your driving test without taking driving lessons first? A selection interview is an important event in your career. Like all important events, it demands preparation. Think about what you want to achieve during the interview, consider what you have to offer the employer and what you want to get from them.

11. **Successful job seekers are well informed about the organisations to which they apply.** Researching the organisation and the job shows that you are keen, proactive and serious about your application. Find out all you can via company reports, publicity material and the Internet. You will use this information during the interview.

12. **Successful job seekers think about their responses before the interview.** You can't rehearse a script for an interview and you can't predict exactly what questions will be asked. What you can do is think about commonly asked questions and how you would answer them. Then you are less likely to be caught unawares and say something you later regret!

13. **Successful job seekers know that first impressions count.** Depending on who you talk to, people sum you up during the first thirty seconds, one minute or four minutes of a meeting. No, it's not fair, but we all do it. So think about your appearance, choose clothes that suit the occasion and walk into the interview confident that you present a positive, professional image.

14. **Successful job seekers practise their verbal communication skills.** We learn to speak when we are children. It is a skill we can continually refine and use to our advantage. During the thirty or forty minutes you spend in the interview room, clear and attractive speech is essential. Listen to people who speak well and try to identify what makes you want to listen to them. Be aware of people whose speech irritates you and pinpoint the problems so you can avoid the same habits.

15. **Successful job seekers know how to listen.** Listening is a much underrated skill. In western cultures we tend to talk, to avoid gaps in conversation and

to be afraid of silence. To understand what other people want from you, you must listen to them. Listening, like speech, is a skill that you can improve.

16. **Successful job seekers understand the basics of non-verbal communication.** This is a complex field and one in which a little knowledge goes a long way. Don't become so obsessed with the concept of 'body language' that you become nervous and self-conscious. At the same time, be aware that stance, gestures and facial expressions are powerful signals. In a face-to-face conversation, non-verbal communication signals say more than words. Avoid irritating habits, put your shoulders back, sit up straight and smile.

17. **Successful job seekers do not make snap decisions.** To be offered a job is a great achievement. You have been selected above all the other candidates, you have proved your worth. However, you still need to take your time to think about the offer. Is this really the job you want? If it is, then accept and celebrate. If you are not sure, then weigh up the pros and cons. Don't accept a job out of desperation, gratitude or a sense of obligation. If you do, you'll be scanning the appointments sections again within six months.

18. **Successful job seekers negotiate the deal they want.** If you are clear in your own mind what you want out of your new job then you are in a strong position to negotiate terms and conditions with your new employer.

Negotiation means that both parties are satisfied with the outcome. Be realistic about what you ask for – and make sure that the employer is realistic about what they require from you. Negotiating a salary and benefits package is an important part of the job-seeking process, so take your time.

19. **Successful job seekers value feedback.** Never be afraid or embarrassed to ask selectors for feedback. They can help you to improve your job-seeking skills by discussing the strengths and weaknesses of your performance. Use their advice positively. It is not a personal criticism but a means of improving your job-seeking skills.

20. **Successful job seekers never stop looking, never stop preparing and never stop following up leads.** Approach your job search systematically and keep up the momentum. Above all, believe that the job you want is out there and that you are going to get it.

USEFUL CONTACTS

Although research suggests that responding to advertisements is not the most successful way to find a job, it is still the method most commonly used. If you are looking for advertised vacancies, consult the broadsheets on the days when they focus on your specialist area or buy them on the days when they do a round-up of jobs as a special supplement.

Appointments supplements are printed on the following days:

Thursday *The Times, Daily Telegraph, Independent*
Saturday *Guardian*
Sunday *The Sunday Times, Sunday Telegraph*

Local papers will usually have a weekly job section. Although many vacancies may be for support and lower grade staff, they are still worth consulting.

Working abroad

If you are looking for a job abroad, contact *Overseas Jobs Express*. Published every two weeks and available on subscription, it focuses on working and living overseas.

Overseas Jobs Express
Premier House
Shoreham Airport
Sussex BN43 5FF

Tel. 01273 440220
web site: www.overseasjobs.com

The Employment Service publishes free fact-sheets about living and working in Europe. These are available from Jobcentres.

You may need to compare your qualifications with those required in the country in which you intend to work. In the European Union, professionals whose training has been regulated by statute, statutory instrument or a professional association under a Royal Charter and require at least three years of degree level training will have their qualifications automatically recognised by Member States. If you need further advice or clarification contact the DfEE

DfEE Qualifications for Work Division (QfW2)
Moorfoot
Sheffield S1 4PQ

Tel. 0114 259 4151

Self-employment

If you decide (as an increasing number of people are now doing) that you want to move out of the job market and into self-employment, there are a number of organisations that can offer valuable advice to help you get started.

Start with your local enterprise agency (the number will be in your local telephone directory) to find details of starter courses and incentives.

Central addresses include:

Business in the Community
44 Baker Street
London W1M 1DH

Tel. 0171 224 1600
web site: www.bitc.org.uk

Business in the Community
c/o European Components Co Ltd
770 Upper Newtownards Road
Dundonald
Belfast BT16 0UL

Tel. 01232 410410

Scottish Business in the Community
30 Hanover Street
Edinburgh EH2 2DR

Tel. 0131 220 3001

Scottish Enterprise
120 Bothwell Street
Glasgow G2 7JP

Tel. 0141 248 2700
web site: www.scotent.co.uk

LEDU, The Small Business Agency
LEDU House
Upper Galwally
Belfast BT8 6TB

Tel. 01232 491031
web site: www.ledu-ni.gor.uk

In Wales, one telephone call to Business Connect will put you in contact with the agencies in your area that can help you establish your business. Call Business Connect on 0345 969798.

The Small Firms and Business Links Division of the DTI produces free booklets to help small businesses. Local Business Link numbers are available on the freephone Signpost Line (0345 567765).

Careers counselling/executive search

Organisations offering a range of careers-related services – including counselling, career evaluation and help in finding unadvertised vacancies – advertise in the national press. Many now have Web sites on the Internet which will give you an outline of their services. Alternatively consult the Yellow Pages for your area.

FURTHER READING

There are dozens of books available from high street book stores on different aspects of the job search. Titles on preparing CVs and letters often give sample formats which you can use as the basis of your own applications. You may also find it useful to look at books on performing well in tests and answering questions during interview. A word of caution; use these books as guidelines. *You* are applying for jobs, not the writer. Nobody can prepare your correspondence, take the tests or answer the questions for you.

Useful points of reference for more detailed information include the following books, which you will find in libraries or business book shops:

Adler, R. B. and Towne, N. (1993, seventh edition) *Looking Out/Looking In*, Harcourt, Brace Jovanovich

Fisher, R., Ury, W. and Patton, B. (1997) *Getting to Yes*, Arrow Business Books

Hodgson, P. and Hodgson, J. (1992) *The Sunday Times Business Skills Series: Effective Meetings*, Century Business

Martin, D. (1996) *Tough Telephoning*, Institute of Management

McIlwee, T. and Roberts, I. (1991) *Human Resource Management*, Elm Publications

Morris, D. (1994) *Bodytalk: A World Guide to Gestures*, Jonathan Cape

Torrington, D., Weightman, J. and Kirsty, J. (1985) *Management Methods*, Gower

INDEX

ability tests 116–17
abstract tests 116
achievements 28, 53, 54, 81, 142–3
action verbs 65–6, 142
active listening 147, 148–9, 186–7
active voice 65
additional information 81
advertisements 3, 34–5, 37, 40–2, 199
   interpreting 55–8
   responding to 59–60, 84
advice 25, 208
age 58
agencies 35, 39
aggressiveness 136, 155, 176
analysis exercise 113–14
application forms 41, 51, 78–82, 200
   letters with 83–6
   templates 35
appointments sections 4, 41, 205
appraisal systems 195
aptitude tests 117
assertiveness 135, 136, 142–3, 175, 176
assessment centres 27, 36, 108–15
attitude 118
authority 22–3
awareness 29

bargaining strategies 176–7
body language
   feedback 185–6
   golden rule 203
   interviews 139, 140, 149, 151–5
   negotiation 176
boredom 155
brevity 63, 69
business awareness 29

chronological CVs 70–4
clarification 145
closed questions 107, 143
closing date 82
clothes 131–3, 202
commitment 15, 17–19
communication, non-verbal
   feedback 185–6
   golden rule 203
   interviews 139, 140, 149, 151–5
   negotiation 176
communication skills
   assessment centres 110, 112, 113
   listening 96, 146–50, 186–7, 202–3
   negotiation 175–7
   telephone 5, 91–7, 183, 201
   verbal 138–43, 176, 202

written 5, 60–91
commuting 164–5
competences 25–9, 53, 54, 75–6
competition 41
compromise 172, 173–4, 178
computers 45–8, 62–3
confidence 95, 126, 131–3, 142–3, 155
  see also assertiveness
consultancy 40
contractual details 165–8
control 29
conventions 66–7
correspondence *see* letters
counselling 25, 208
covering letters 45, 61–7, 82, 83–91, 200–1
cultural values 153
CVs 41, 51, 67–78, 200
  feedback 184, 187, 188
  Internet 46, 47
  templates 35

databank 6–7, 29, 52–5, 79, 189
decision making 110, 113–14
defensiveness 155
determination 15–16
direct approaches 44–5
  see also speculative letters
direction 29
discussions, group 112
drafting 62
dress style 131–3, 202

editing 64–5
education 54, 72, 123
effectiveness 28
emotions 13–14, 185
employment agencies 35, 39
employment history 54, 72–3, 122–3
employment trends 30–1
enterprise agencies 206–7
enthusiasm 94, 95
executive search 34, 37, 40, 208
exercises 27, 110–14
experience-based CVs 70, 76–7
expert advice 25, 208
expertise 28
extra curricular activities 55, 74

feedback 119, 179–88, 204
first impressions 131–3, 134–5, 202
flexibility 11, 28
focus 69
follow-up letters 89
format, letters 85
functional CVs 70, 75–6

golden rules 6, 199–204
graduate salaries 171, 172

group discussions 110, 112
groups, assessment centres 108–15
The Guardian 41, 46

headhunters 34, 37, 40
hours 22, 167
humour 137–8

ideal job profile 20–4
in tray exercises 110, 111
industry norms 170
influence 29
initial contact 4–5, 51–98
  advertisements 55–60
  telephone skills 91–7
  written skills 60–91
    application forms 78–82
    CVs 67–78
    letters 61–7, 82, 83–91
intellectual requirements 34
interest 155
internal recruitment 37, 38–9, 195
Internet 41, 44, 45–8, 121, 172, 208
interpersonal skills 28, 109
interpreting advertisements 55–8
interviews 5, 36, 101–58, 201, 202
  assessment centres 108–15
  feedback 179–88
  listening skills 146–50
  non-verbal communication 139, 140, 149, 151–5
  questions 107, 124–9, 137, 143–6
  research 120–31
  skills 131–8
  speech 138–43
  tests 115–19
Investors in People 37

job analysis 33, 36
job description 31, 33, 34, 45–6, 81, 84, 122
job-related competences 25–6, 27, 53, 54
journals 40, 41

keeping records 189–90
  see also personal databank

labour market trends 30–1
language 62, 64, 65–6
layout, CVs 68
leading questions 107, 144
length, CVs 69
letters 45, 61–7, 82, 83–91, 200–1
listening skills 96, 146–50, 186–7, 202–3
location 22, 164–5, 170–1
Lockett, John 19–20, 25, 44
logical error 105

management 26
Management Charter Initiative 26

market trends 30–1
mirroring 104–5
mobility 195
modesty 126
mood 94–5
motivation 28

negative postures 152
negotiation 112, 170–9, 203–4
nervousness 155
networking 42–4, 89, 199
newspapers 4, 40–1
non-verbal communication *see* communication, non-verbal
notes 6–7
numerical tests 117, 118

objectivity 13–14, 184–5
occupational competences 25–6, 27, 53, 54
offers 161, 162–79
on-line recruitment 44, 45–8
open questions 107, 144
opportunities 23
organisation characteristics 23
organisational skills 111
outplacement consultancy 40
overseas jobs 205–6

panel interviews 105–6
passivity 136, 176
pay *see* salary
person specification 34, 35, 58, 70, 110
personal competences 26–7, 53, 54
personal databank 6–7, 29, 52–5, 79, 189
personal details 73–4
personal development 17, 123–4
personality 34, 157
personality tests 116, 117, 118
persuasion 28
physical requirements 34
Plan Your Career 19–20
positive postures 152
Powerful Networking 44
practicalities 163–5
prediction 148
preoccupation 147–8
preselection 35, 36, 39, 78, 102–3
presentation 63, 68
prioritising 111
probing questions 144–5
problem-solving 109, 112, 113, 117
professional advice 25, 208
professional journals 40, 41
professional qualifications 54, 58
profile 71–2
promotion 38
psychology 152–3
psychometric testing 119
publications 73

qualifications 54, 58, 171, 206
questionnaires
  ideal job profile 21–4
job-seeking 14–15
  questions 107, 124–9, 137, 143–6

rarity value 171
reasoning 29
recent performance 171
recognition 24
record-keeping 189–90
  see also personal databank
recruitment process 4, 30–5, 37–48, 51–2, 59, 199
Reed International 47
referees 74
rejection 179–88
relocation 165
remuneration *see* salary
requirements 34
research 44–5, 52, 120–31, 201
responsibilities 21–2, 54
Reviewing Your Career 25
role plays 110, 112–13
The Rules 6, 199–204

salary 21, 166, 167, 170–9, 204
selection 4, 30–2, 35–6, 51–2, 59, 199
  see also interviews
  application forms 78–9
  assessment centres 108–9
  competences 26–7
  tests 115–16
self-assessment 27–9
self-employment 206–7
sequential interviews 106
sexism 66
sideways movement 38–9
simulation exercises 27, 112–13
skills 75–6, 115–16, 122
  see also communication: competences
social contacts 42–4, 89
speculative letters 86–9
  see also letters
speech 138–43, 202
spelling 62–3
statistics 30
stress 135
style, CVs 68–9
subconscious 152–3
subjectivity 51–2, 104
superficiality 105
systematic approach 19–20

targeting 18, 44, 87
team working 110, 112
technology 11, 30
telephone contact 5, 51, 59–60, 88–9, 91–7, 183, 201
tests 110, 115–19

time 22
timing
  feedback 183
  job offers 168
  telephone calls 93–4
  tests 118–19
training 16, 54, 123
transferable skills 26
travelling 164–5

unwilling job seekers 13–14

verbal communication 138–43, 176, 202
verbal reasoning exercises 116–17
vocabulary 62, 64
voice tone 139–40, 141–2

working abroad 205–6
working environment 134, 163
written communication skills 5, 60–91

Yellow Pages 44, 208